Bernhard Schulz

The Reichstag

The Parliament Building
by Norman Foster

Foreword
Wolfgang Thierse

Preface
Norman Foster

Bernhard Schulz # The Reichstag

The Parliament Building by Norman Foster

Prestel

Munich · London · New York

Previous page:
The Reichstag at night with its new glass cupola aglow.

Front cover:
View of the Reichstag,
photo: Richard Bryant/Arcaid

Back cover:
Interior view of the dome,
photo: Dennis Gilbert /View

Library of Congress Cataloguing-in-Publication is available.

Die Deutsche Bibliothek –
CIP Cataloguing-in-Publication-Data.
A catalogue record for this publication is available from Die Deutsche Bibliothek

© 2000 Prestel Verlag,
Munich · London · New York

© of works illustrated by the artists, their heirs or assigns, with the exception of works by: Joseph Beuys, Christian Boltanski, Enrique Roman Carrazoni, and Katharina Sieverding bei VG Bild-Kunst, Bonn 1999; by Christo 1995.

Prestel Verlag
Mandlstrasse 26, 80802 Munich, Germany
Tel. +49 (089) 38 17 09-0
Fax +49 (089) 38 17 09-35;
175 Fifth Avenue, Suite 402, New York,
NY 10010
Tel. +1 (646) 602-8616,
Fax +1 (646) 602-8639; and
4 Bloomsbury Place, London WC1A 2QA
Tel. +44 (0171) 323-5004
Fax +44 (0171) 636-8004

Prestel books are available worldwide. Please contact your nearest bookseller or write to any of the above addresses for details concerning your local distributor.

Editing: Philippa Baker and
Katharina Wurm
Translation from the German:
Peter Green
Design and typesetting:
Norbert Dinkel, Munich
Lithography: Eurocrom 4, Villorba, Italy
Printing: Aumüllerdruck, Regensburg
Binding: Conzella, Munich

Printed in Germany
Printed on acid-free paper

ISBN 3-7913-2184-6 (German edition)
ISBN 3-7913-2153-6 (English edition)

Photo Credits:
Bildarchiv Preussischer Kulturbesitz, Berlin 20; Bilderdienst Süddeutscher Verlag 27 left; Bryant, Richard/Arcaid Front cover, 11, 15, 37, 65, 67, 68, 72, 76, 77, 78 (2), 81, 82, 87, 90, 103, 110; Bundesbaugesellschaft, Berlin 34; Bundesbildstelle Bonn 30/31; Carrazoni, Enrique 116/117; Gilbert, Dennis/View back cover, 4, 12/13, 24/25, 42/43, 54/55, 63 top, 71, 73, 79, 86, 88, 91, 94, 100/101, 108; Görner, Reinhard 80 top; Hellmann, Dieter 104 top; Landesbildstelle Berlin 28; Meisel, Rudi/Visum 17, 80 bottom, 96/97, 112/113; Das Reichstagsgebäude in Berlin Westermann Verlag, Braunschweig 1987 (Originally published in Leipzig 1897): 21, 22/23; Voller Ernst, Berlin 27 right; Volz, Wolfgang 38; Ward, Andrew 114; Wulf, Reimer 48; Young, Nigel/Foster & Partners frontispiece, 6, 18, 29, 61, 62, 63 bottom, 64, 69, 70 (3), 74, 75, 83, 84/85, 89, 92, 93, 95, 102, 104 bottom, 106 (2), 107 (2)

Contents

Foreword
7 Wolfgang Thierse

Preface
9 Norman Foster

16 **Introduction**

The History of the Reichstag
19 Early Developments
19 Paul Wallot's Design

The History of Parliamentary Government in Germany
23 Imperial Age
26 Weimar Republic
26 Nazi Germany before 1939
26 Second World War
27 Post-War Period

The Conversion Plans
30 Moving the Capital
31 The Architectural Competition
35 The Cupola Debate

39 **Intermezzo: Christo's**
Wrapped Reichstag

Foster's Conversion Scheme
40 Basic Design Principles
41 The Exterior
46 Spatial Layout
56 Access and Circulation
60 The Conservation Concept
66 The Interiors
78 Art in the Reichstag
86 The Debating Chamber
92 The Roof Terrace and Cupola
104 The Energy Concept

The Reichstag in the German Capital
109 The Parliamentary and Government District

111 **The Reichstag as a Symbol of German Unity**

114 **Biography Norman Foster**

115 **Bibliography**

116 **Facts and Figures**

118 **Foster and Partners** Project Team
119 Consultants
119 Suppliers and Subcontractors

The mirrored cone, sun-screen and spiral ramps inside the cupola.

Foreword

Wolfgang Thierse,
President of the German Bundestag

The view at night from the eastern portico through to the chamber and the federal eagle.

After a 66-year-long interruption the German Bundestag resumed work in the Reichstag building in Berlin on 19 April 1999. The move to this building was an historic moment which turned the Reichstag into the permanent seat of the German parliament and Berlin into the political capital.

However, both the move from the Rhine to the Spree and the building itself were the centre of some controversy in the past. The Reichstag building was frequently referred to as a symbol. A symbol of what? Of the Wilhelminian era? Of the downfall of the Weimar Republic? Of the Hitler regime? Of the division and reunification of Germany?

Don't the walls still exude the spirit of the Wilhelminian era? Isn't it actually an architectural landmark of its time?—with its mixture of styles which Tilmann Buddensieg mockingly referred to as "synthetic Imperial", a mixture of elements from the Italian Renaissance, Neo-Baroque and—in the case of the old dome—the combination of steel and glass. Although Friedrich III and Wilhelm I both had a hand in the building's later development, it was Kaiser Wilhelm II who laid the foundation stone in 1884. However, it did not go unnoticed by critics that more members of the military were present at the ceremony than members of parliament.

Nevertheless it would be wrong to stress this identification with the Imperial era too much. When the building was completed in the late 1890s, the Kaiser publicly referred to it as "the epitome of bad taste",

he harassed the architect Paul Wallot and, in correspondence, described the structure as an "empire ape house".

The building and the decisions taken in it were more closely orientated on parliamentarian democracy than restorationist absolutism. Outstanding parliamentarians on both sides of the political system, such as Rudolf von Bennigsen, Eugen Richter, Wilhelm von Kardorff, Ludwig Windthorst, Matthias Erzberger, August Bebel and Friedrich Ebert, were involved in debates on the colonial issue or on establishing a naval fleet, on the 'ludicrously dangerous ambitions of the Social Democrats' or the peace agreement of 1917.

Even so, the Reichstag of the Empire did not succeed in changing the constitution in favour of extended rights for parliament. It was therefore fitting that Philipp Scheidemann proclaimed the first republic from one of the windows of this building on 9 November 1918. At last the country was to have a democratic constitution and the Reichstag became a forum for parliamentary debate.

Unfortunately it did not become a symbol for untroubled parliamentarianism. Soon after the 1920 election, the expression "republic without republicans" was coined. The Great Depression of the 1920s marked the beginning of the end of the first democratic period in Germany.

Despite this, one of the most stubborn prejudices associated with the Reichstag building still remains;

namely that it is a symbol of the horrors of National Socialism, its racial persecution and war politics.

None of this is true. Adolf Hitler never spoke in this building as a parliamentarian. In fact, it was only after the Reichstag had been set on fire in 1933 that the National Socialists replaced the "compassionate morality" of the democratic state with their own theory of the "German master race". It was in the provisional parliamentary chamber in the Kroll Opera House and not in the Reichstag that the Enabling Act was passed, abolishing the basic rights anchored in the Weimar constitution and facilitating the persecution and arrest of political adversaries.

The Reichstag building survived the war. It stood as a memorial for future generations, particularly after the construction of the Berlin Wall, directly fronting this artificial, enforced border that separated East and West. Simply its height alone meant that it could not be overlooked. For many people in East Berlin, the Reichstag building became a symbol for the unresolved issue of a divided German nation. It was the architectural symbol of the longing for a united Germany in which democracy, peace, personal liberty and social justice would be able to exist side by side.

Of course, the Reichstag is a symbol. But an ambiguous one. It is a symbol for all the ambivalence and ambiguity of German history which we Germans can only accept as such and have to accept in its entirety.

The fruitful interconnection of old and new, of past and present is particularly evident in architecture. It is thanks to the architect Norman Foster that both the interior and exterior of the building meet our expectations, that on entering one feels welcomed rather than overwhelmed.

With his concept of integrating a new plenary chamber and a new dome into the existing historic structure he has achieved a successful synthesis. It reflects the building's history, its present and its future with architectural means. Norman Foster has made history visible— but not only that. At the same time he has created space both for democratic structures and for the workings of parliament. We owe Norman Foster our gratitude for his excellent design.

This book makes the impressive modern architecture of the revamped Reichstag accessible to visitors and helps them to get to know it.

I hope that many interested visitors from Germany and abroad will come and visit the German Bundestag in the new Reichstag building and will explore its fascinating architecture with the help of this book.

Wolfgang Thierse

A sketch made by Norman Foster during his first site visit in July 1992.

Preface
Norman Foster

The Reichstag has witnessed almost every major public gathering in post-war Berlin, from protest rallies to rock concerts. The project that we submitted in the first round of the Reichstag competition, in 1992, responded to that tradition by placing the Reichstag at the heart of a public forum, sheltered beneath a roof umbrella that symbolically tied together the old and the new. This roof also worked ecologically, har-

vesting energy, directing light into the Reichstag's interiors and aiding a system of natural ventilation.

However, with the adoption of the Spreebogen masterplan in 1993, our brief for the second round of the competition changed dramatically and the accommodation required was reduced to a point where it could easily be fitted within the shell of the existing building. Rather than adapt our scheme, we began again from first principles. We started with a building whose mutilated symbolism meant little to most Germans. The simplest approach would have been to scoop out the interiors and insert a modern structure in their place. But we grew to understand that history still resonated through the Reichstag's fabric and that it should not be swept away.

Our transformation is therefore rooted in four interconnected issues:

the significance of the Bundestag as one of the world's great democratic forums; a determination to make Parliament more accessible to the public; a passionate commitment to producing an exemplary low-energy, environmentally friendly building; and a respect for history as a force that shapes buildings as well as the life of nations.

The Reichstag bears the imprint of time and events more powerfully than any exhibition. As we peeled away the plasterboard and asbestos that had lined the interiors of the 1960s rebuilding, the bones of the old Reichstag came to light, along with striking imprints of the past, including nineteenth-century mouldings, the scars of war and the graffiti left by victorious Soviet soldiers in 1945. Preserving these traces allows the building to become a living museum. Junctions between new and existing work have been carefully articulated to allow the different layers in this historical "palimpsest" to be read and understood.

The reconstructed building feels new in spirit but when appropriate it takes cues from the old Reichstag. In planning the new rooms, for example, we have been guided by the subtleties of axial door and window alignments. More fundamentally, we have reinstated the original entry sequence up the grand flight of steps from the west and restored the chamber to its original orientation. People entering the building can now look directly into the chamber towards the seats of the President of the Bundestag, the

Chancellor and other national leaders.

In other ways, however, our approach represents a radical departure. Originally the Reichstag was compartmentalised and highly stratified. We have gouged through these layers from top to bottom, opening up the building to light and views. This is most apparent in the chamber where MPs can look up directly to the cupola, the highest point of which is more than 40 metres, the equivalent of thirteen domestic storeys, above their heads.

For MPs the chamber is the natural focus of the building, but members of the public also come there to listen to debates. It is important that they should feel involved in this process. The chamber and public tribunes are therefore designed to create an intimate relationship between public and politicians.

Beyond the chamber are spaces that form part of the parliamentary machinery. A key consideration for us was encouraging activity within the building even when Parliament is not in session. We argued successfully that the faction rooms—party meeting rooms—should be housed in the Reichstag and not located in neighbouring buildings as originally intended. Alongside them on the third floor are the press lobby and bar, which look down onto the activity in the chamber below.

The introduction of works of art into many of these spaces represents another layer in the Reichstag's evolving history. The Reichstag is one of Germany's most remarkable public art projects. Twenty artists were commissioned to create works to hang in the committee rooms and major public spaces, most of them site specific, and artists were free to work to any scale and on any theme. The Reichstag is thus a museum of memories and an extraordinary gallery of contemporary art.

In designing the interiors our first instinct was that a parliament building should have *gravitas*. We devised a colour strategy using a muted palette that we planned to apply only to the doors, using it to differentiate floor levels and groups of related activities. However, at a crucial Building Committee meeting led by former Chancellor Helmut Kohl, that strategy was overturned. Committee members were adamant that younger generations would expect to see bright, welcoming, colourful interiors. As a result, we invited the Danish designer Per Arnoldi to explore with us the use of dynamic colour on the panelling in the principal public rooms. The effect is occasionally startling but it offers a vivid counterpoint to the buff monotone of the exterior or the quiet presence of the new stone floors.

It is above these working levels, on the roof terrace and in the cupola, that the public realm reasserts itself. I have described the results of our transformation as radical. Where else in the world can politicians and visitors walk together as equals through the main ceremonial entrance of their national Parliament building, rise to a plaza on the roof, look down into the main

Left:
The historical stone portico seen through the new glass west façade.

Following page:
The cupola—a popular symbol of the new Berlin.

assembly chamber below, continue by ramps to a viewing platform, or meet for a coffee or a meal? As former Bundestag President Rita Süssmuth observed: "The citizens are literally encouraged to climb on-to our roof."

When the question of a new cupola was first raised, there were powerful voices in favour of rebuilding the historical dome. I was passionately opposed to that idea. But I understood that the Reichstag ought in some way to signal its transformation on the Berlin skyline, communicating the themes of lightness, transparency and public access that underscore the project. We conceived the new cupola as a "lantern", with all the associations that term implies.

The cupola is symbolic of the process of "lightening" that the old building has undergone. Crucially, however, it is also an integral working part of the building and a key component in our light and energy-

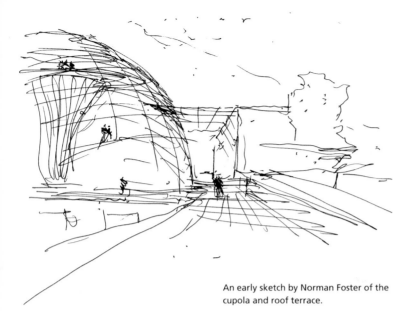

An early sketch by Norman Foster of the cupola and roof terrace.

saving strategies. At its core a "light sculptor", a mirrored cone that works like a lighthouse in reverse, reflects daylight from a 360 degree horizon down into the chamber. A moveable shield tracks a path around the cone, blocking solar gain and glare while allowing sunlight to dapple the chamber floor. The cone also aids the chamber's natural ventilation system, extracting warm air at high level.

In energy terms the Reichstag offers a model for the future. Germany has led Europe in its environmental and energy-related legislation, and from the outset our aim was to demonstrate the potential for a wholly sustainable public building. The fossil-fuel burning services installed in the Reichstag in the 1960s emitted an alarming 7000 tonnes of carbon dioxide annually. We swept away those installations

and developed a radical new solution, using renewable "bio-diesel"—refined vegetable oil from rape or sunflower seeds. When vegetable oil is burned in a co-generator to produce electricity it is remarkably clean and efficient compared to traditional fuels. Heating and cooling the building now produces an estimated 440 tonnes of carbon dioxide per annum—a 94 per cent improvement.

The Reichstag's own demands are now so modest that it has become a net producer of energy, performing as a local power station for the new parliamentary quarter. And rather than waste the heat generated by its power plant, it is able to store it for future use. In summer, surplus hot water is diverted into a natural aquifer 300 metres below the ground. In winter, this water can be pumped up to heat the building, or to drive

an absorption cooling plant that produces cold water. This is also stored below ground, in a shallower aquifer, and can be pumped back into the building in hot weather to provide cooling via chilled ceilings: nothing is wasted.

In its vision of a public architecture that redresses the ecological balance, providing rather than consuming energy, lies one of the Reichstag's intrinsic expressions of optimism. It is optimistic also in another sense: as night falls and the glass bubble of the cupola glows, the building becomes a beacon, signalling the strength and vigour of the German democratic process.

Fourteen architects from across Europe, the United States and Japan were invited to take part in the first Reichstag competition. It is surely a sign of a progressive, open society that it can contemplate appointing a foreign architect to build its national Parliament building, and can then work with him, and a host of other consultants from around the world, to realise that vision. My colleagues and I feel privileged to have taken part in that process and to have helped the Reichstag to its rebirth.

Norman Foster

The light-reflecting mirrored cone—both a light sculptor and a sculpture in its own right.

Introduction

On 19 April 1999, Berlin's public institutions held open house and tens of thousands of people queued to take their first look at the interior of the refurbished Reichstag building. The streams of visitors have not abated since and all the optimistic predictions have proved true: the Reichstag has become a favourite with the public. Not only the notoriously inquisitive citizens of Berlin, but the ever-growing number of visitors to the city are drawn to the building, which has become an absolute must in any sightseeing tour. The view from the extensive roof terrace is one of the most spectacular in the "new" capital, and this alone would be enough to maintain the building's attractiveness for the foreseeable future. However, there is much more to the Reichstag than that.

People are always searching for symbols—especially symbols of the intangible—and far more quickly than was ever expected, the glazed cupola of the Reichstag building has become a symbol. First and foremost, it stands for the German Parliament, the Bundestag, which has now taken up permanent residence in the Reichstag. The transparency of the glass cupola communicates the Bundestag's decision to be an institution open to observation and regulation and one that in fact calls upon the electorate, which it serves, to exercise these functions.

In addition to this, the new cupola is associated with the "Berlin Republic", a vague term, certainly, but a significant one. The expression "Weimar Republic" was exposed to the constant contempt of the National Socialists. Not even its adherents could remember Germany's first parliamentary democracy without recalling its weaknesses. But the Weimar Republic had no architectural symbol. Weimar was merely the place where the Republic was founded, not the scene of its everyday political life for its fourteen years of existence, from 1919–33. Its activities were in fact concentrated in the Reichstag.

If the Berlin Republic is the generic expression for a reunified Germany with a parliamentary democracy, the process of moving the functions of political rule from Bonn to Berlin is distilled in the Reichstag's cupola. What is more, it represents the much longer process of the growing together of the two German states, which were forcibly divided for forty years.

It was rightly recognised that a reunified Germany would have stronger roots in history than the two German states founded after the Second World War—the Federal Republic of Germany and the German Democratic Republic. For the roots from which German unity grew go back far beyond 1945. They reach back at least to the time of the Weimar Republic, in which the Reichstag came to assume its full political significance. The image of the new glass cupola, therefore, incorporates this dual aspect of German unity: recalling its roots in the past on the one hand; and pointing to its new future on the other. Perhaps it is these references that have allowed the new cupola to become such an undisputed symbol of a new era of German history.

A stream of visitors snaking up the spiralling ramps of the cupola.

The light new interior of the Reichstag, clearly
visible at night through the historical west portico.

The History of the Reichstag

Early Developments

The decision to make the Reichstag building the seat of the modern German Bundestag was a consequence of its parliamentary history. But how were the location and formal design of the original building determined? Not in the manner of countries such as England, where the use of a historical palace was the obvious solution; in Berlin, no such building was available. Nor in the same way as the United States of America, where parliamentary buildings were given fitting locations as part of a masterplan for the new capital of the new country.

The founding of the German Empire under the aegis of Bismarck came about relatively suddenly and caught the Prussian capital unprepared. The creation of imperial institutions was in its infancy when a place of assembly had to be found for the newly established Parliament, the Reichstag. As early as the spring of 1871, only a few months after the founding of the German Empire, a parliamentary building commission was constituted with the ambitious task of finding a site, drawing up a programme of construction, and holding an architectural competition for the assembly hall.

The process dragged on fruitlessly for a long time, and in the meantime a makeshift solution was devised. Bismarck took up his work as Chancellor of the Reich before a Parliament that convened in hastily converted, provisional quarters in the Leipziger Strasse. When his responsibilities ended with his dismissal in 1890, the same temporary accommodation was still in use.

At first, the realization of a home for the Reichstag proceeded smoothly enough. The site chosen was on the eastern side of the Königsplatz, a huge square in the west of the city, some 300 x 200 metres in extent. On the west side of the Königsplatz was "Kroll's Etablissement", a large restaurant that in its later guise as an opera house was to play a disastrous role in German parliamentary history. On the east side, the proposed site of the Reichstag, was the palace of Athanasius Raczynski, a Polish count from Poznan. With the foundation of the German Reich, this area—like the entire so-called "old" west of the city—increased considerably in value, since many wealthy citizens and a number of prestigious institutions such as the Prussian general staff established themselves here.

The architectural competition for the Reichstag building was held in 1872. It is worth stressing that this competition was an international one: no fewer than fifteen architects from England alone participated, and the second prize was awarded to Sir George Gilbert Scott, the leading representative of the Neo-Gothic style and architect of numerous churches. With the declaration of Ludwig Bohnstedt as winner, all that was necessary for work to begin was that the site should be made available. But Count Raczynski, whose permission had not been sought, refused to hand over his property and all work ground to a halt.

Only in 1881 was agreement reached on the use of the site. A second competition was now necessary, not least because the spatial requirements had been revised and more precisely defined. The centrepiece of the complex was to be the debating chamber, which was to accommodate 400 representatives and have an area of 600 square metres. The jury had to judge between more than 189 entries from competitors "of the German tongue", as specified in the brief. Two first prizes were awarded: to Friedrich Thiersch, whose star as an academic teacher was in the ascendant, especially in Munich; and to Paul Wallot from Frankfurt/Main. Wallot was finally awarded the commission in 1882.

Paul Wallot's Design

Wallot's original design had to be substantially revised and underwent a number of alterations in the course of construction. When the

The laying of the Reichstag's foundation stone by Kaiser Wilhelm I in 1884.

foundation stone was laid in 1884, all that was determined was that the debating chamber should be in the eastern part of the building and that there should be a monumental approach from the west via a vestibule.

Stylistically, the Reichstag is unique. Its attribution to the all-embracing historicist style of the end of the 19th century is useful only as an initial point of reference. In fact, Wallot adopted neither canonised Renaissance models nor those of the High Baroque, which was just coming back into vogue at the time, but rather employed various stylistic forms to create something entirely original, namely a "synthetic imperial style", of which the Reichstag has since been regarded as the sole example. From today's point of view, it is difficult to understand the protracted discussion that took place over the style of the building. At the time of its inception, however, each historical style was associated with a specific meaning: Romanesque architecture, for example, was regarded as a symbol of the imperial grandeur of the Holy Roman Empire; the Renaissance, in contrast, was seen as bourgeois, since it had its origins in the Italian city republics; while the Baroque style was considered courtly. Last, but not least, a distinction had to be made between north and south, between the Protestant and Catholic states of Germany.

The task of creating a highly symbolic building for the newly united empire under Prussian leadership therefore required a thorough knowledge of historical building forms. Wallot possessed this knowledge and knew how to apply it in masterly manner without committing himself to a specific style and thereby alienating the adherents of other stylistic forms. In modern Berlin, where most of the historical fabric—especially public buildings—has been destroyed by the ravages of war and post-war demolition, it is scarcely possible any more to draw the comparisons that would show just how unique the Reichstag building really is. This applies in particular to the domed High-Baroque urban palace built by Andreas Schlüter in 1707 as the seat of the Prussian King and German Kaiser, from which the Reichstag building had to distinguish itself externally as the seat of Parliament.

The dome was considered vital to the overall effect of the Reichstag. Its position was not determined by practical factors such as the need to bring daylight into the chamber but by aesthetic ones such as achieving harmonious proportions in the overall appearance of the building, and creating a suitably grand impression at close quarters and from a distance.

The dome originally designed by Wallot bore little resemblance to the size and form of the structure ultimately executed. Due to the interference of the Building Commission and Kaiser Wilhelm I, the dome was constructed not from stone as Wallot had intended but from glass and steel, it was made smaller and its position was changed twice.

It was not a dome at all in the

sense of a spherical shell: it had a deviant vaulted form known as a domical or polygonal cloister vault.

In 1888 Kaiser Wilhelm I died and his son, Friedrich III, was succeeded after only three months by Wilhelm II. He, like his predecessor, meddled with Wallot's design. The young Kaiser's choice of the austere Baroque style of Andreas Schlüter as his aesthetic standard simply made it more difficult to achieve a stylistic balance in the Prussian-dominated capital of the Reich.

Although the Reichstag is often described as Wilhelmine in its expression of imperial pomp, Wilhelm II himself, who opened the building in 1894, privately derided it as the *Reichsaffenhaus* or "Imperial Ape House". Not only did it represent the growing sovereignty of the people, but its dome dared to be higher than the Berlin Stadtschloss.

The plan of the main level or *piano nobile* of the original Reichstag by Paul Wallot.

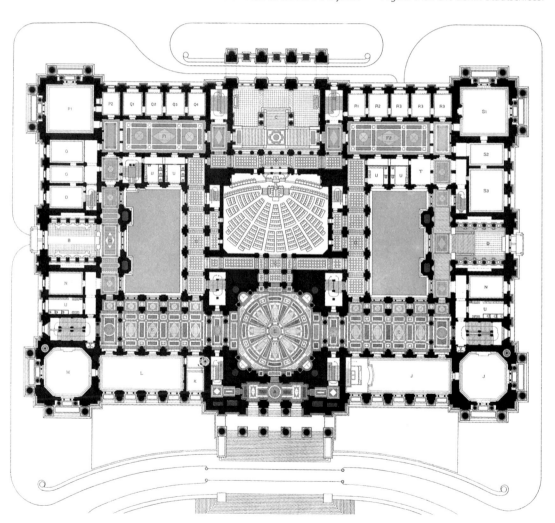

A drawing of the west elevation of the
Reichstag on its completion in 1894.

Following page:
The restored grand west entrance where public and politicians enter the building together.

The History of Parliamentary Government in Germany

Imperial Age

The significance of the powerful appearance of the Reichstag building to the development and consolidation of parliamentary democracy in Germany should not be underestimated. It was none other than the representatives of social democracy, so resolutely opposed by Bismarck, who advocated a design worthy of the importance of the National Assembly. Only a generation after the abortive revolution of 1848, the idea of popular parliamentary representation was overshadowed by that of the nation state. However, during the reign of Wilhelm II, the Reichstag assumed increasing importance as a national stage. Even if the empire was not imbued with the true spirit of a parliamentary system, the Reichstag knew how to carve out a place for itself as a counterforce to the Kaiser and the court, and indeed to the government and the influential military. Its increasing significance is reflected in the decision to extend the building with the addition of an extra floor of offices in 1912. Just how much the political balance had begun to shift during the First World War is illustrated by the inscription *Dem Deutschen Volke* (To The German People) which was afixed to the western pediment in 1916, after two decades of resistance from the Kaiser, who objected to its egalitarian sentiment. Although it was finally inscribed to galvanise the nation during the dark days of the First World War, the

dedication was originally intended to transcend all ranks and classes of society and thus epitomise the process of democratisation in the German Reich.

Weimar Republic

The Reichstag—the assembly and the building in which it convened—experienced its greatest, its true period as a Parliament during the Weimar Republic. This had its beginning in Berlin when, on 9 November 1918, Philipp Scheidemann proclaimed a German Republic from a window on the west façade of the Reichstag building. This announcement was the outcome of the disastrous developments of the final autumn of the war in 1918, and sparked a revolution that threw Berlin into months of turmoil and street-fighting. The election of a National Assembly on 19 January 1919, which met in the relative calm of Weimar to draw up a new constitution, marks the beginning of the first era of true parliamentary democracy in Germany. The Reichstag convened again in Berlin only in August 1919. Its house remained in much the same form that it had survived the Imperial Age.

However, the increased number of delegates and the change from an assembly of representatives to a Parliament with various parties and groupings, revealed the inadequacies of the building. Paul Löbe, the long-serving President of the Reichstag and later the President by seniority of the first German Bundestag in 1949, aptly described these deficiencies by remarking that the

Reichstag offered "a great deal of space, but little room". But attempts to extend the building in the course of the next few years, especially through the addition of a new space for the library, came to nothing.

Nazi Germany before 1939

The entry of the NSDAP Brownshirts into the Reichstag marks the beginning of the end of the Weimar Republic. The uniformed Nazi delegates made no secret of their contempt for democracy. Although an increasing bitterness tainted its activities as the Nazi Party gradually gained power during the 1920s, Parliament continued to function in the Reichstag. However, by the time the debating chamber went up in flames on 27 February 1933, and the burning dome became a symbol of the downfall of democracy and constitutional government, Hitler and his strong-arm men had already painfully curtailed the powers of Parliament. The formal elimination of constitutional government through the Act of Enablement, drawn up on the following day, took place shortly afterwards.

In March 1933 the Reichstag delegates, already vastly depleted in number as a result of the persecution of various Members, gathered in the Kroll Opera House to give their blessing to the abandonment of the Republic. Henceforth, the Reichstag became a puppet assembly. Until the early days of the Second World War it convened in the Kroll Opera only nineteen times, to cheer the speeches of Adolf Hitler, the Führer and Chancellor of the Third

Reich, and to sing the party anthem, the "Horst Wessel Song". With their typically dry humour, the citizens of Berlin described it as "the world's most expensive choral society".

The Reichstag's dome was reglazed and the building made watertight in order that it could house propaganda exhibitions such as *The Bolshevik Terror* and *The Eternal Jew*, but the debating chamber was left untouched. However, Hitler and his architect Albert Speer planned to retain the building as the library to a vast new assembly hall with a 290-metre-diameter dome, and to route their hypertrophied North-South Axis past it as part of the proposed rebuilding of Berlin as "Germania".

Second World War

The Reichstag was not to play a central role again until the final phase of the battle for Berlin. For most of the war the building was not used at all by the Nazi regime, but rather served as a military medical library where casualties on the front were recorded, and as a makeshift mater-

Left:
The inscription *Dem Deutschen Volke* (To The German People) being installed over the Reichstag's west portico in 1916.

Right:
Yevgeny Khaldei's famous photograph of the raising of the Red Flag over the Reichstag in 1945.

nity ward. However, strangely enough, at the end of April 1945, the Red Army concentrated its efforts to capture the centre of Berlin, which was still in the hands of the German Wehrmacht, entirely on the burnt-out Reichstag. The fact that Stalin viewed the Reichstag as a symbol of Nazi rule is perhaps attributable to the fire of 1933 which was blamed on the Communists. That the building was not used by the Nazi regime seems to have escaped his attention.

For decades, photos showing Red Army soldiers raising the Communist flag on the roof of the Reichstag were thought to capture the moment of Soviet victory over Hitler's Germany. Only a few years ago, however, a statement by the photographer, Yevgeny Khaldei, revealed that his photos show a re-enactment, staged two days after the real event, to create a propaganda image for Stalin.

In the aftermath of the battle the sandstone blocks of the Reichstag were covered with the graffiti of

Soviet soldiers celebrating their victory. The symbol of parliamentary democracy was turned into a symbol of the Soviet triumph over Hitler.

Post-War Period

During the post-war period there were more urgent problems to consider than the reuse of the burnt-out Reichstag. At least the building had survived. Its position on the boundary between two districts of Berlin, which now formed the border between the Soviet and British zones of occupation, also meant that the building was left to its fate. However, it became the backdrop for many public events. In 1948, hundreds of thousands of Berliners gathered in front of the ruined building to hear Mayor Ernst Reuter's famous words against the Soviet blockade of West Berlin: "Peoples of the world, heed this city!" The next year Germany split into two parts, East and West, and the Western capital moved to Bonn.

During the 1950s the vague designation of the Reichstag as a

Left:
The battered shell of the Reichstag after the Second World War.

Right:
The west portico of the restored Reichstag in 1999.

More than ten million visitors saw this exhibition in the course of the two decades it was on show. With it, they also saw important parts of a building intended to reflect the modern political face of the Federal Republic of Germany, in the same way that the parliamentary buildings in Bonn did.

In 1987–88, when the Federal Republic of Germany had long come to terms with its provisional capital in Bonn and had commissioned extensive projects including a new, improved debating chamber for the Bundestag, the House Committee decided to explore the possibility of rebuilding the Reichstag dome.

Then, unexpectedly, in 1989, the Soviet Empire in Eastern Europe collapsed and the Berlin Wall was torn down. German reunification suddenly became a reality. For the first time since 1933 the Reichstag could be used for its true purpose. On 4 October 1990, the day after reunification came into effect, the general assembly of the Bundestag met in the Reichstag. On 20 December of the same year, the Twelfth Legislative Period of the Bundestag assembled there as the first freely elected Parliament of Germany.

future seat of Parliament for a reunified Germany merely reflected the general state of bemusement in German politics of the time. The more the division of the country became an established fact, the less realistic any use of the building as a Parliament became. A competition for its reconstruction, opened at the beginning of 1960 by the Minister for Current Affairs, referred to the building simply as a "meeting place". This set in motion the long and never fully resolved problem of the non-use or alternative use of the Reichstag in the shadow of the Berlin Wall. The Wall, built in 1961 immediately outside the eastern entrance of the building, sealed the division of Germany and marked the edge of East Berlin as the capital of the Soviet-backed German Democratic Republic.

In the shadow of the Wall, the rebuilding of the Reichstag went ahead in the hands of Paul Baumgarten in 1961. Ten years later the

work was completed without any great ado. Over the years, it had become a fully equipped parliamentary building—with the exception of the fixed seating in the debating chamber. However, according to the Quadripartite agreement of 1971, as long as Germany was divided, the Reichstag building could be used by the Bundestag only for party and committee meetings and for issues specifically related to Berlin. The occasional meetings of various Bundestag committees that were held there merely made the silence in which the Reichstag slumbered on the edge of the Tiergarten all the more evident.

However, the Reichstag gained considerable popularity through the unexpected success of the exhibition *Questions of German History,* which had initially been planned as a temporary event. The exhibition was opened on 18 January 1971, the 100th anniversary of the foundation of the Second German Empire.

The Conversion Plans

Moving the Capital

The context in which discussions took place in 1990–91, for the location of the capital of the reunified country, may be described, briefly, as follows. As a historical legacy of German parliamentary rule, the Reichstag building played no overt part in the debate about the future capital of Germany and the decision taken on 20 June 1991 in favour of Berlin. Once the decision had been made, however, the choice of the Reichstag as the new home of the Bundestag was a logical conclusion. The "seat of the German Bundestag is Berlin" was a key statement in the decision on the capital; and five months later, it was identified by the Bundestag's Council of Elders, with their choice of the Wallot building. Shortly afterwards, in April 1992, an architectural competition for the conversion of the Reichstag building to accommodate the German Bundestag was announced.

The brief for the new architectural competition required that the building "meet the functional, spatial and design needs of a modern working Parliament". A key sentence read: "The design should exhibit transparency, expressing accessibility to the public and a sense of pleasure in communication, discussion and openness." Baumgarten's

conversion was considered to fall short of these requirements. Ultimately, everyone agreed that the Reichstag should be given a new architectural appearance.

However the memory of the Wallot building was like a portent of an ill omen. Opponents of the removal of the capital to Berlin painted a picture of the relapse of a chastened country into a state of unpredictable nationalism, for which the Reichstag would provide the backdrop. The counterpoint to this —the image of a modern democracy firmly rooted in Western values— was symbolised by the debating chamber in Bonn by Günter Behnisch,

completed in 1992. Here, all the rhetoric of transparency and accessibility to the public was spelt out.

The course of the new competition can be understood only in the context of this tension between an acknowledgement of German history, inherent in the choice of the Reichstag building, and the fear of this history, which disqualified the adoption of any symbolism and formal language of the past. The participants were given a precisely defined spatial programme; but the answer to the key issue—how the Reichstag should be treated as a historic monument—was left entirely to the architects and planners. Furthermore, the question of the urban integration of the building into a future structure of parliamentary and government buildings in the area was left open. This problem was to be resolved in an international urban planning competition for the Spreebogen held in parallel with the architectural competition.

The Architectural Competition
The 1992 competition resulted in February 1993 in the announcement of three equal prize-winners. The thinking behind this was that the three quite different schemes made "important contributions to the discussion that was expected to take place between the client and the public about the role Parliament was to play and the image it wished to project". The presentation of the three winning schemes, by Norman Foster from Britain, Santiago Calatrava, a Spanish architect based in Switzerland, and Pi de Bruijn from

The west façade after the 1960s restoration with much of its ornamentation eliminated and the dome destroyed.

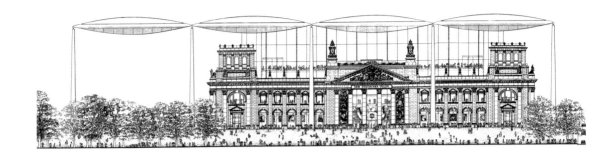

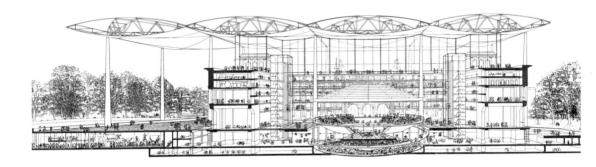

Top:
A drawing of the Reichstag's west elevation for Foster's first competition scheme of 1992–93: the building was placed under a huge sheltering and energy-harvesting roof.

Bottom:
A sectional perspective view of the "big roof" scheme looking north into the chamber.

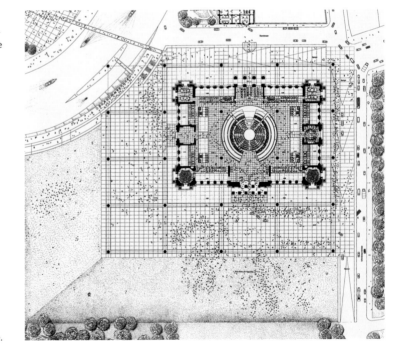

Right:
The plan of the first competition scheme.

A model of Foster's first competition scheme showing the Reichstag from the north bank of the River Spree.

the Netherlands, did indeed spark the discussion anew. But there was another reason why a definitive scheme had not been chosen. The results of the Spreebogen competition were announced alongside those of the Reichstag competition. The winners were Axel Schultes and Charlotte Frank from Berlin. Their evocative design, in the form of a linear complex—a "Federal Strip" that twice spanned the River Spree—reactivated the whole discussion.

Schultes' proposals for the location of buildings for the various ancillary functions of the Bundestag next to the Reichstag and to the north of it obviated the need to squeeze all the functions into the converted historical structure. The

Reichstag building stands to one side of this urban strip, and it was evident that the reordering established by Schultes' federal mile precluded too free a treatment of the Reichstag building. Pi de Bruijn's idea of moving the debating chamber to a new structure in front of the historical building proved unacceptable for this reason, quite apart from other functional reservations. The same applied to Norman Foster's initial design, which proposed spanning the entire Wallot building with a separate roof structure that would have extended asymmetrically at the sides.

Immediately after the announcement of both sets of competition results, all three Reichstag prizewinners were asked to revise their

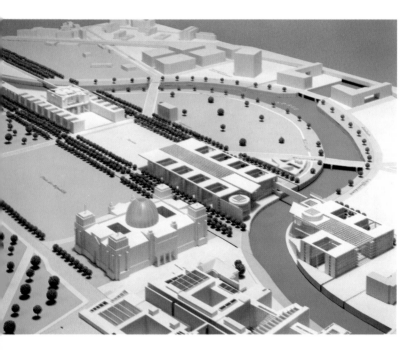

Opposite page, top to bottom:
A design sketch by Norman Foster of the Reichstag's cupola with the key features of the final structure in place—rounded top, spiral ramps and mirrored cone.

A sketch by Norman Foster showing early ideas for the light-reflecting cone.

Another option for the roof-top feature —a response to requests for a more rounded "dome-like" structure.

schemes. The outcome was surprising. Two of the three practices dropped fundamental aspects of their original designs: De Bruijn abandoned the idea of a separate debating chamber, and Foster dispensed with the separate roof. Foster made no bones about the fundamental revision of his scheme and wrote that it was necessary to start again from a new beginning.

The effort paid off, for in June 1993, the parliamentary advisory committee to the Bundestag decided to award the commission for the further planning of the work to Foster. The key points of his new concept, which also found public approval, were the respect shown for the historical structure; the emphasis placed on the debating chamber through its central location within the building and transparent

A model of Axel Schultes and Charlotte Frank's masterplan for a new parliamentary quarter in Berlin, which conflicted with the first Reichstag competition schemes.

Foster's preferred option for a roof-top structure—a glazed drum capped by a disc-shaped wind scoop, known as the "lighthouse".

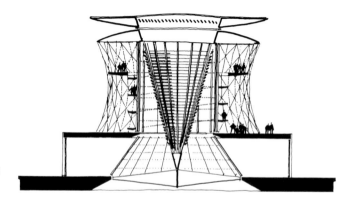

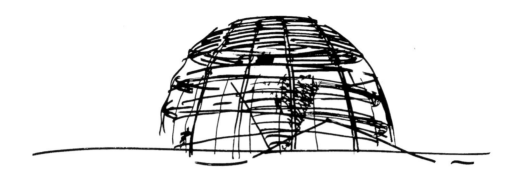

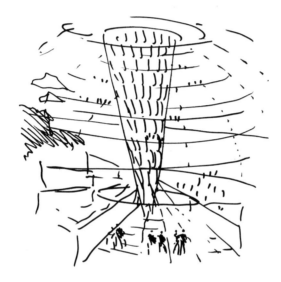

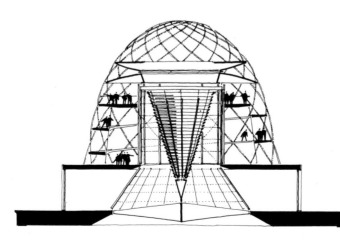

walls; the environment-friendly agenda and the commitment to public accessibility, with the roof level dedicated to the public.

The Cupola Debate

Having won the competition, one of the first problems that Foster encountered was that of the dome. The question of the dome had been answered decades before by the architect Hans Scharoun in his own inimitable way. After studying the designs for the reconstruction of the dome in the 1960 competition, he remained silent for a long time before finally saying just one word: "Why?" By this time, no part of the original dome existed. The burnt-out steel framework had been demolished in November 1954 on the pretext that it was in danger of collapsing; and at that time there was no thought of ever rebuilding it.

Scharoun's "Why?" expresses the dominant reaction in the new discussion that took place after Foster was awarded the commission in June 1993. The original rejection of a historical reconstruction of Wallot's dome was questioned on a number of occasions. Wildly con-

flicting statements were made by experts about the costs and the effects of the dome on the design of the debating chamber and its lighting, none of which helped in reaching a conclusion.

The politico-aesthetic controversy revolved around the symbolic content of a dome. Opponents of the dome saw in it an expression of the reactionary, arrogant behaviour of the past. For them, it was a sign pointing in the wrong direction. Supporters, on the other hand, referred to it as a symbol of the former sovereignty of the people. On more than one occasion, Norman Foster himself made it clear that he was not prepared to reinstate the dome in its historical form, seeing this to be an empty historicist gesture fundamentally at odds with the whole ethos of his scheme. He stressed the underlying idea of mak-

ing the roof accessible to the public and the debating chamber visible from above. As an alternative to a dome, Foster suggested a cylindrical glazed lantern as a fitting symbol for an open democracy and a forward-looking nation.

In compliance with the Bundestag's wish for a dome, Norman Foster sought a solution in harmony with his design concept and sketched numerous lanterns that might top the building. In the early part of 1995, a choice was finally made from a large number of designs. The concept selected, showing a rounded glazed cupola with double-spiral access ramps on the inside, is the one now implemented.

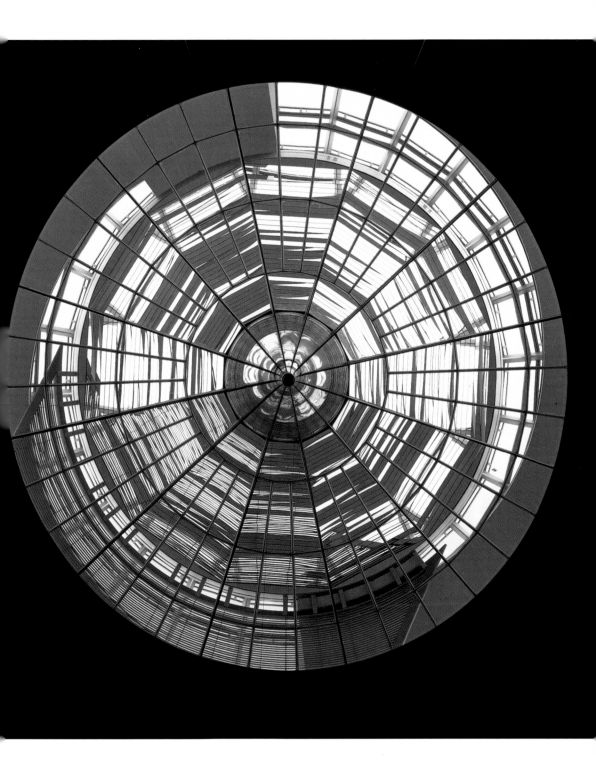

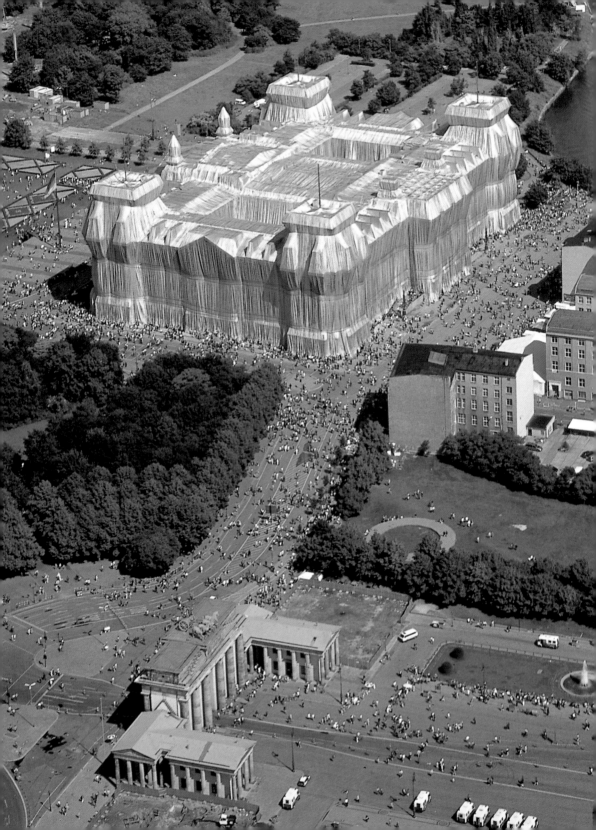

Intermezzo:
Christo's *Wrapped Reichstag*

The wrapping of the Reichstag by the artist Christo and his wife Jeanne-Claude in late June and early July 1995, was a moving public event and marked the turning point from the tricky negotiation and decision-making of the design stage to the actual reconstruction work. Controversy over this project, which the artist had conceived twenty-five years before and which enjoyed considerable support in the media, posed a greater problem for the Bundestag than the actual conversion of the building. The debate in the house on Christo's project in February 1994 was a remarkable exception to everyday parliamentary activity: for the first time in the history of the Federal Republic of Germany, Members of Parliament debated an artistic project.

The fears for the "dignity of the house" voiced at that meeting evaporated into thin air in the face of the festive and happy atmosphere that the implementation of Christo's concept brought to Wallot's building, indeed, to the entire city. Millions of people came to admire the silent spectacle of light and colour, movement and shadow. The transformation of a colossus darkened with age into a bright silvery sculpture put an end in the eyes of the public to the unthinking association of the building with an ill-fated German past. In the image of the good-humoured masses gathered around the *Wrapped Reichstag*, the community recognised itself, at least for a brief carefree moment, as a modern society with a future, a society that had learned to come to terms with its past in an enlightened manner.

It was this same image that Norman Foster's design sought to express in the language of architecture. "Christo's *Wrapped Reichstag*", Foster recalls, "was somehow cathartic. It seemed to unburden the building of its more tragic associations and prepare it for the next phase of its career." As soon as the last strips of fabric were removed from the Reichstag on 7 July 1995, the conversion of the building into the seat of the German Bundestag began.

An aerial view of the Reichstag during the *Wrapped Reichstag* project by Christo and Jeanne-Claude in late June and early July 1995.

39

Basic Design Principles

Events behind the fence around the construction site from 1995 onwards became a focus of public attention, not only for the media, but for the numerous tourists who were able to observe the work from the outside and, on occasion, recognise certain key features, without being aware of the unifying concept underlying it all. On 19 April 1999, the moment had come. Exactly on schedule, the Bundestag was able to hold its first working meeting in the new debating chamber. Norman Foster handed the symbolic key of the building to Wolfgang Thierse, the new President of the Bundestag who had succeeded Rita Süssmuth. In the days following the political "consecration" of the Reichstag, the electorate and visitors to the city took possession of the building: like no other Parliament building before it, the converted Reichstag is accessible to them as well as their elected representatives. This quality of openness was planned by Foster from the very beginning and remained an important aspect at all stages of the design.

What exactly has Foster achieved? The building is neither completely new nor merely a restored historical edifice. It is a combination of old and new. This was a condition of the brief issued by the client, the German Bundestag. When Foster accepted the commission to carry out the work, priority was attached to three main principles: in terms of its construction, the conversion was to meet the demands of a modern working parliament; secondly, it was to take account of historical links, without adopting an historicist approach to the building; and thirdly, the design was to be environment friendly and oriented to the future. The first principle related to the functional needs of the client, the German Bundestag. The second was a purely architectural issue. The third principle involved the mechanical services in the broadest sense of the term—an area that is coming to assume ever greater importance in construction today: technical infrastructure, energy supply and the interaction between the building and its environment. Achieving a synthesis between these three factors is something that the Foster office has long pursued in projects of increasing complexity, including the construction of the largest enclosed space ever constructed, Hong Kong International Airport. In this respect, the architect's design is in the best tradition of Paul Wallot, whose building was remarkably progressive and technically advanced for its time. The bold engineering feat represented by the cupola is merely the most visible token of this.

Norman Foster has defined four thematic areas that influenced the rebuilding: "a belief in the significance of the Bundestag as one of the great democratic forums of the world"; "making the process of government more accessible to the public"; "an understanding of history as a force that shapes buildings as well as the lives of nations"; and, finally, "a passionate commitment to the low-energy, environment-friendly agenda which is

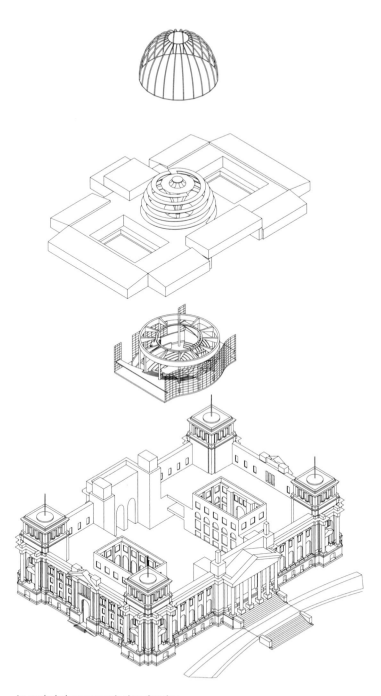

An exploded axonometric view showing
how the new chamber and third-floor level
were slotted into the shell of the old Reichstag.

fundamental to the architecture of the future". In the architect's own words, with the construction of the new building, he wished "to transform a famous national monument, full of melancholy and stirring memories, into an optimistic symbol both of the new Germany and the new Europe".

The Exterior

A visitor approaching the Reichstag, who has perhaps caught a glimpse of the glass cupola from a distance, is confronted with what, at first sight, may seem to be a confusing building: a modern glass cupola is set on top of a massive nineteenth-century stone structure. The principal façade, the western elevation, is oriented to the square in front of it, where the Victory Column and a monument to Bismarck once stood. On completion of the extensive rail and road transport links and the erection of a tall flag-pole to the right, this public open space will be given only a restrained landscaping treatment.

The most striking elements of the stone shell of the building are the powerful colonnaded Corinthian portico in the middle of the west façade and the square corner towers, which provide a visual counterweight to the cupola and establish a rhythmic sequence in the outline of the building. Massive semi-circular pilasters projecting from the façade extend over the height of the two principal storeys, which are articulated by the form of the windows. Set in front of the façade at the corners of the building

are independent columns which echo those of the portico. They support an elaborate entablature, above which the tower structures rise. The fine original reliefs on both sides of the portico have survived. They contain depictions of the coats of arms of the German states at the time of the Second Empire and are in the form of a genealogical tree, surmounted by the octagonal crown of the Holy Roman Empire. Since the time of the Habsburg emperors, however, this crown has had its home in Vienna, not in Berlin.

By comparison, the north and south façades are relatively unelaborate, with relief ornamentation in the form of piers and a crowning architrave over the entrance portal. The eastern façade, facing the city centre, is quite unique. The vehicular approach is contained within a broad projecting central bay, which takes the form of a modified triumphal arch with a window above it on the second main floor level. The overall impression of this projecting structure is angular, brusque, almost forbidding.

The basis of Wallot's synthetic imperial style with its repertoire of Baroque, Neo-Baroque and Renaissance forms is still visible: the symmetrical façades; the pilasters and columns with plinths and capitals; the window openings crowned by triangular or segmentally curved

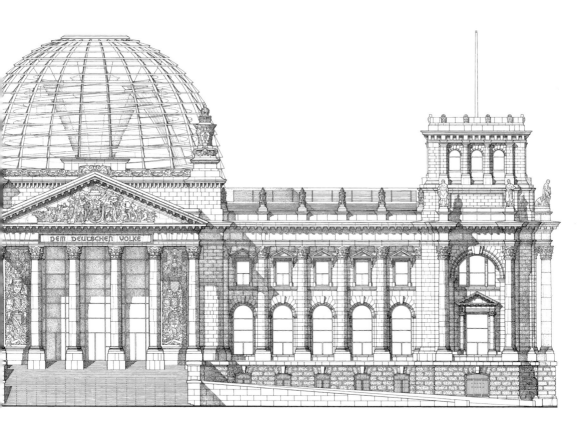

DEM DEUTSCHEN VOLKE

A drawing of the west elevation of the new Reichstag: the old stone façades remain but above them the new glass cupola signals the building's transformation.

pediments; the vertical division into a rusticated stone plinth, a two-storey main section accentuated by monumental columns and pilasters, and an attic zone above the entablature; and finally, the richly decorative forms.

These exteriors were nearly all that remained of Wallot's original building when Foster and Partners began work on the Reichstag. Although much of the building's internal fabric was damaged by the fire of 1933 and the bombardment of the Second World War, it would still have been possible to restore it when Baumgarten started reconstruction work in the 1960s. However, Baumgarten did his utmost to

keep the historical magnificence of the building at bay, in keeping with his times.

In Baumgarten's rebuilding the interior was completely gutted and vast quantities of masonry were removed in order to create a more "democratic" and open building. The façades were conserved but also "purified"; in other words they were stripped of much of their decoration. What survived of the historical fabric was disguised with a lining of plasterboard. Not a single wall, let alone the rich ornamentation, remained visible. The final building had 21 committee rooms, 200 offices and a debating chamber with space for 650 MPs but much of the internal logic of Wallot's original was lost: for example, corridors were built across the internal courtyards. Finally, Wallot's storey divisions were abandoned in response to the need to create large spaces that went far beyond the formal spatial programme of the original building. This was not attributable to Paul Baumgarten alone; to a large extent, it occurred at the instigation of civil servants of the federal building administration. The superbly cleaned exterior of Wallot's building now presents itself in the purified and simplified form that characterised the stylistic mood of its time.

In his scheme, Foster has left the façades unchanged, but added a new dominant element in the form of the glass cupola. The democratic inscription, *Dem Deutschen Volke*, has survived, becoming a signal for the future as much as a memory of the past. The room-height fenestration to the west façade has also been retained and carries Baumgarten's concept over to the present. What Foster's ideas and those of his predecessor Baumgarten have in common is the theme of extensive transparency.

Spatial Layout

In a public building of this kind, which is in constant use by hundreds, sometimes thousands of people, two fundamental issues have to be resolved: the spatial layout and the circulation. Visitors are usually unaware of these matters. What is important for them is a swift and simple means of navigation. It was important, therefore, to articulate and arrange the spaces of the Reichstag building in a comprehensible manner.

The planning revolved around the most important space in the building: the debating chamber. The original Wallot structure provided an enlightened solution to the location of the chamber: it was placed at the centre of the building, not only because this was the most suitable space for the large area required, but because the chamber had to be seen as the heart of the parliamentary process.

Symbolic considerations such as these are certainly open to debate. Etymologically, the word Parliament means talking place, which is why it is linguistic nonsense to try to distinguish a talking Parliament from a working Parliament. Speaking in the debating chamber, however, is no longer the main activity of the Members. Only in Britain perhaps does a classical kind of Parliament still exist where pointed speeches are made and a spontaneous process of decision-making on the part of Members takes place.

From the very beginning in Germany, the representatives were, and are to an increasing extent, experts in various fields. They rely on the support of their own assistants, on a highly qualified research unit, and not least on the library. Today's Members of Parliament bring their specialist knowledge to bear both on committees, where they help to formulate bills and to control "their" ministry, and within their own party and working groups.

Opposite page, top to bottom:
Comparative east-west cross-sections looking north through the Wallot, Baumgarten and Foster schemes respectively. Baumgarten removed Wallot's heavy, compartmentalising walls and introduced horizontal layers. The Foster scheme cuts through these layers to make the Reichstag light and open.

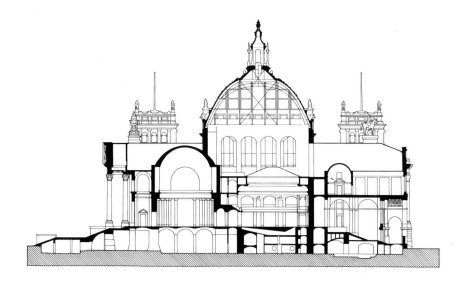

1894 Wallot

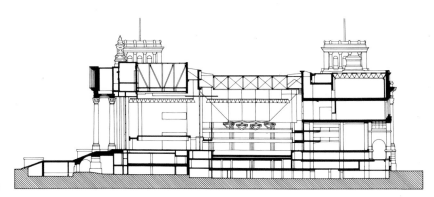

1971 Baumgarten

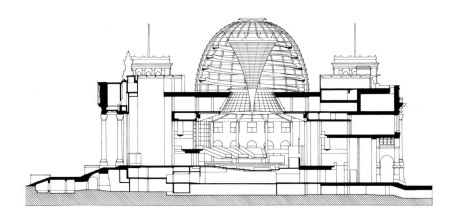

1999 Foster

Left:
An aerial view of the Reichstag with
the Schultes-Frank "Federal Strip" under
construction to the north.

Below:
A plan of the Reichstag and the Platz
der Republik showing the Schultes-Frank
Spreebogen masterplan.

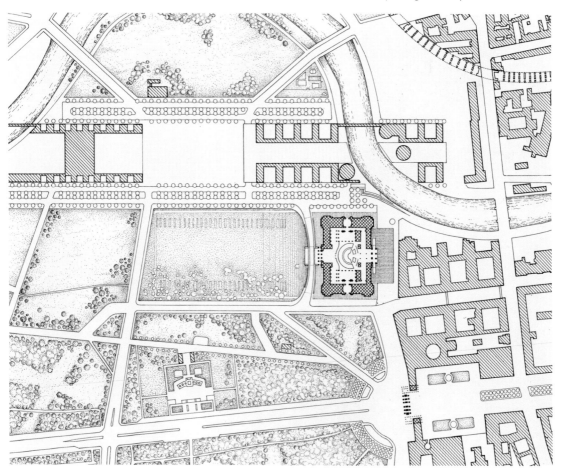

For this reason, the original competition brief of 1992–93 for the conversion of the Reichstag building attached particular importance to providing the necessary administrative and support spaces for the various parties. These could not possibly have been accommodated exclusively within the walls of the existing structure, which was why most of the competition entries proposed additional buildings. The situation was changed fundamentally with the publication of Axel Schul-tes' "Federal Strip" concept which located elsewhere much of the accommodation originally intended for the Reichstag. This allowed Foster to realise his basic concept of transparency and organisational simplicity in a natural and effective way.

Foster, like Wallot, made the debating chamber the most important space on the principal floor of the Reichstag, but here the comparison with Wallot ends. Foster's chamber is as transparent as Wallot's was

Opposite page, top to bottom:
A north-south cross-section through the new Reichstag: the chamber occupies the full width of the plan between the two courtyards.

The plan of the first floor or *piano nobile* —the principal parliamentary level.

Below:
The plan of the ground floor of the new Reichstag, where all the services are housed.

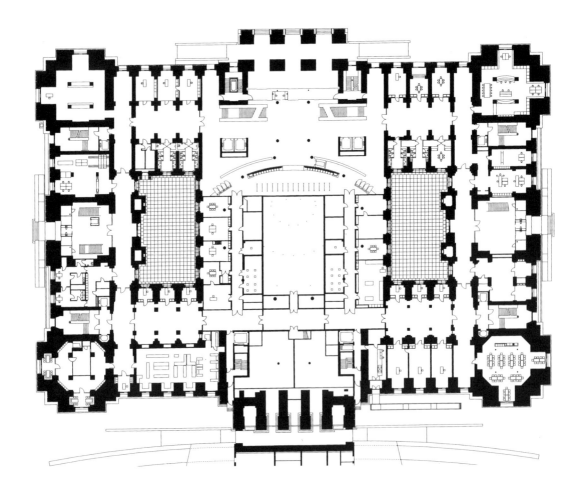

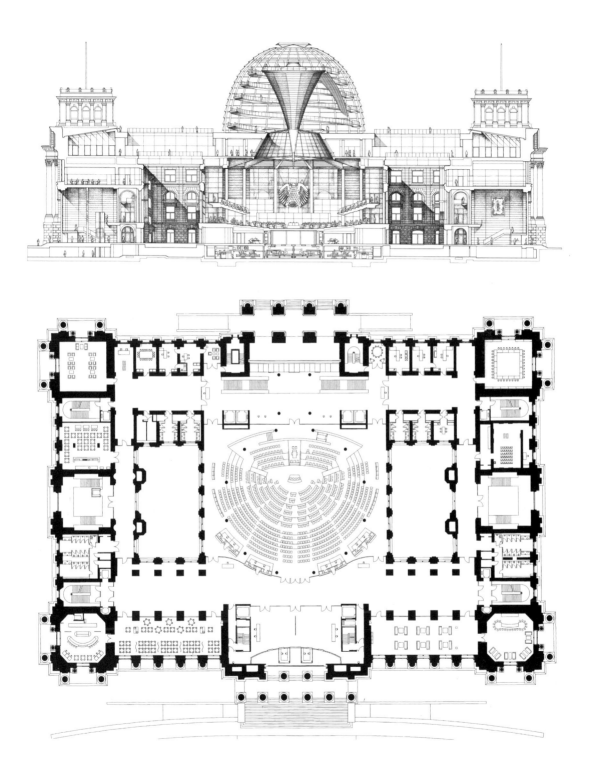

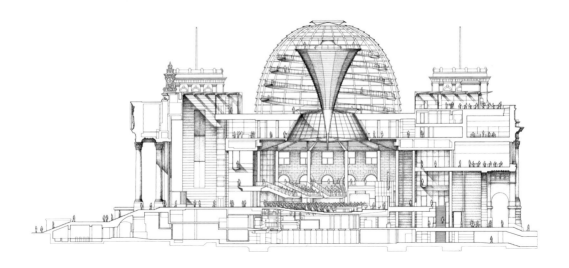

opaque: where Foster's west lobby is oriented entirely to the events in the debating chamber, not only through its location, but by virtue of its glass walls, Wallot had located a magnificent octagonal foyer here, from which the visitor had no perception of the debating chamber beyond.

Foster wanted not only horizontal transparency, affording a view into the debating chamber from the public entrance and from the eastern entrance area reserved for Bundestag Members and employees, but also vertical transparency. His concept of allowing people to look into the debating chamber from the roof, which is a fully public area, was foreseen in the first "big roof" scheme. What Foster wanted was an opportunity for the public to "keep an eye on the Members" in the positive sense of the term. Not all representatives felt comfortable with the notion of having their activities subjected to visual control by

the public, but most agreed that openness and accessibility were fundamental.

Achieving vertical transparency meant that there could be no space of any kind on the upper floors that would restrict the view into the debating chamber or the lighting of this space. The chamber occupies the full width of the plan between Wallot's two courtyards; previously cluttered with corridors, they have been restored to their original purpose. All ancillary functions—offices and committee rooms—are located around the edge of the building with unimpeded views out. On the second floor there are a number of additional working spaces oriented to the internal courtyards. Only the party committee and conference rooms on the third floor, a new level built behind the parapets of Wallot's façades have no external views. At this height, it was not possible to cut window openings in the façade, since the third floor is situated at

Above:
An east-west cross-section looking north showing the strong vertical emphasis of the chamber.

Pages 54–55:
The view through the transparent wall of the chamber from the west lobby at mezzanine level.

the level of the tall attic wall, and so they are top-lit through mono-pitched glazed roofs.

The principal parliamentary and public entry level now forms a *piano nobile* above a ground-level floor of services installations, as it did in Wallot's original plan. At mezzanine level are the public tribunes in the chamber. The second floor is the presidential level, with offices and formal rooms allocated to the President of the Bundestag and the Council of Elders. On the third floor the different parties have their of-fices, while around the glazed soffit of the chamber a broad ambulatory is open to journalists in the press lobby. On top of all these working levels, the public realm reasserts it-self in the great roof terrace which leads to the entry points to the glass cupola, and the restaurant where Members of Parliament and the public can dine together.

Below:
The plan at mezzanine level where the public has access to the tribunes in the chamber.

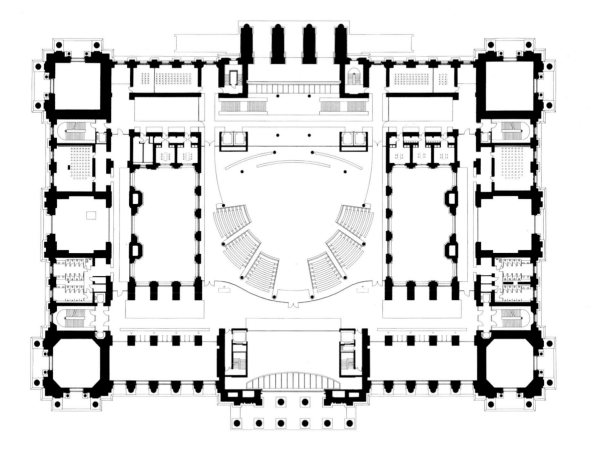

Access and Circulation

Access to the various floors and rooms has been designed in a clear and straightforward manner. Circulation patterns have been defined for three categories of users: Members of the Bundestag and their assistants; journalists; and visitors. Sometimes these groups are kept apart and sometimes they are brought together so that private and public spaces alternate and overlap.

One of the key features of the new circulation system is that Wallot's entry sequence has been restored. In Baumgarten's reconstruction the debating chamber was turned 180 degrees to face west, and the lines of access and circulation were completely changed. The ceremonial western entrance was closed and replaced by less conspicuous entrances in the sides of the building below the *piano nobile* level. Foster has restored the podium to its original position to the east and reopened the western entrance at the top of its grand flight of stairs, which means that those entering the building are confronted

The plan of the second floor—the presidential level.

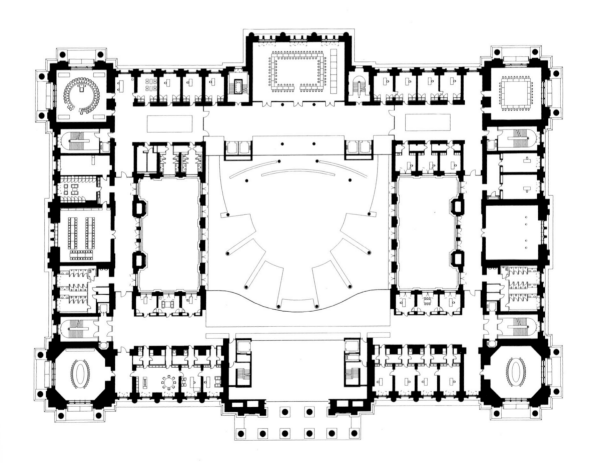

through glazed partitions, with a direct view through to the seats of the President of the Bundestag, the Chancellor and other national leaders. This entrance is open to everybody, so public and politicians now enter the building together as equals by the same route.

From here MPs enter the floor of the chamber or branch off to reception rooms and Members' dining rooms. The main focus of interest for the general public, apart from attending parliamentary debates, will be the roof and cupola. Here,

too, the routes are laid out very clearly. From the lobby they are directed to glass-fronted lifts which ascend to the roof through the entire spectacular height of this daylit western hall. The roof is the realm of the electorate. From here, visitors have a view of the city and of the cupola in the middle, inviting them to ascend to the viewing platform at the top. The lifts also provide access to the tribunes on the mezzanine. At this level, bridges allow the public to circulate in the same corridors as the politicians.

The plan at third floor level: this level was built behind the parapet of Wallot's façades and houses the faction rooms and press lobby.

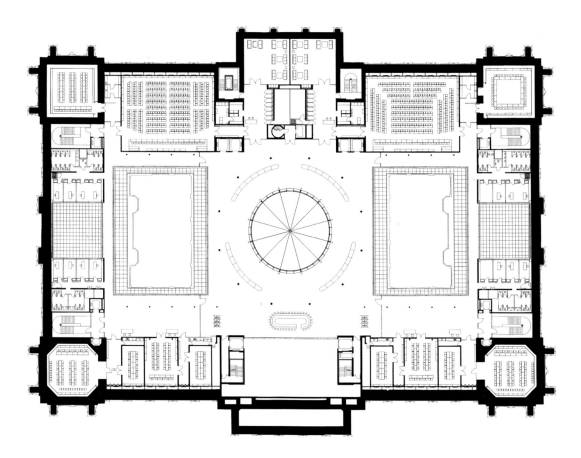

The entrance for Members is situated on the eastern side, the former "city" face with road and tram access. The street, the Friedrich-Ebert-Strasse, which will be renamed the Ebert-Platz at this point, still has to regain its urban significance after being impassable for half a century. From the east lobby, two single-flight staircases lead up to the level of the debating chamber providing a close view of the back of the eagle. The eastern lobby radiates a sense of bustling activity. Members have quick access to the working areas via lifts parallel to the sides of the debating chamber. One of the two linking tunnels to the Members' offices in the Jakob Kaiser building ends in the basement, so that the greatest density of traffic may be expected here and the lifts are sized accordingly.

Members and their assistants can also use the side entrances at street level in the north and south façades, from where staircases lead to the principal parliamentary level with access to the debating chamber.

Below:
The plan at roof level—the principal public level.

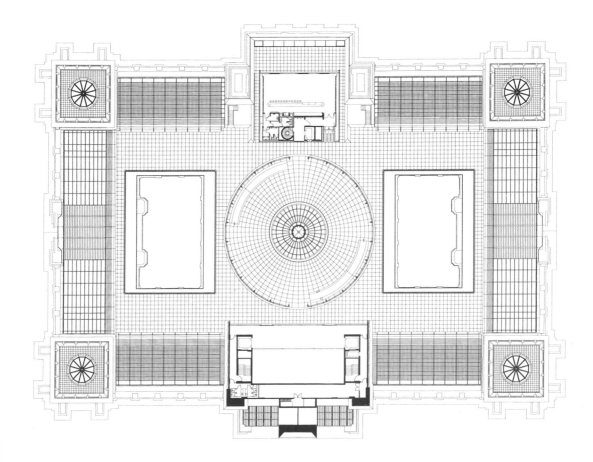

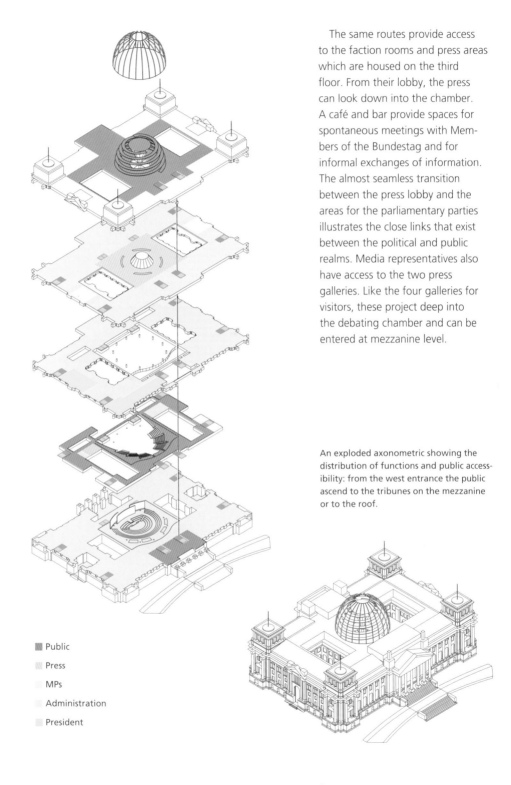

The same routes provide access to the faction rooms and press areas which are housed on the third floor. From their lobby, the press can look down into the chamber. A café and bar provide spaces for spontaneous meetings with Members of the Bundestag and for informal exchanges of information. The almost seamless transition between the press lobby and the areas for the parliamentary parties illustrates the close links that exist between the political and public realms. Media representatives also have access to the two press galleries. Like the four galleries for visitors, these project deep into the debating chamber and can be entered at mezzanine level.

An exploded axonometric showing the distribution of functions and public accessibility: from the west entrance the public ascend to the tribunes on the mezzanine or to the roof.

■ Public

Press

MPs

Administration

President

The Conservation Concept

The historical fabric of the building called for a responsible approach to the heritage of the past and its treatment was probably the most difficult aspect of the conversion. Although the Reichstag has long been listed as a building of historical interest worthy of preservation, it was necessary to clarify in detail what exactly was protected by this status. On the one hand, any construction measure represented an interference with the fabric, the sole exception being Christo's *Wrapped Reichstag* project, which was carried out without a single plug being inserted into the walls. But with the installation of permanent fittings, such scrupulous treatment of the building was not possible. The special problem in the case of the Reichstag, however, was that the extent of the surviving historical fabric was ascertained only when later additions were removed prior to construction work. Up to that point, the building was known purely in the form of the conversion carried out by Baumgarten in the 1960s.

The "lining" of Baumgarten's interiors has now been expunged from the Reichstag. Like most buildings dating from the 1960s and 70s, Baumgarten's interiors had been sprayed with asbestos. This represented a health hazard and the only remedy was to remove all the elements that had been inserted. When Norman Foster peeled away the plasterboard and asbestos lining, the bones of Wallot's Reichstag came to light along with traces of the past that had been hidden for

thirty years. Attention was focused on the original fabric of the building and the decision was made to preserve the marks of history including the damage caused by the 1960s conversion. This was achieved perhaps most impressively in the north and south corridors along the outside of the courtyards. Gradually, the beauty of Wallot's barrel vaulting came to light, and this can now be studied to particular advantage from the slenderly dimensioned pedestrian bridges inserted at mezzanine level. The fact that the projecting ornaments were struck off in the past to allow plasterboard to be fixed to the masonry is also clearly evident.

Among the striking features of the interior are the numerous inscriptions in Cyrillic letters that appear to be freshly applied to the pale sandstone surfaces; they are graffiti written on the walls by Red Army soldiers after the conquest of Berlin in 1945. Those by soldiers are in charcoal; those by officers are in blue crayon. The message "Moscow—Berlin" can be seen in many places: an expression of the long road to victory over Hitler. The date that the battle for the Reichstag really ended—2.5.45—appears frequently, as does 9.5.45, the first day after Germany signed the unconditional surrender to the Allies in Karlshorst. Among the innumerable names recorded here are some of German origin: the ancestors of a certain "Anton Schmitt", for example, may well have been brought to Russia by Catherine the Great.

A decision was made to retain a number of areas of graffiti. The inscriptions have been conserved by specialists who developed new techniques to preserve the Reichstag's past. The Soviet occupation of Berlin and the battle for the Reichstag represent important episodes, even if they were only passing phases in the long and varied history that has left its marks on this building. However, the suggestion of Russian-born artist Ilya Kabakov that a golden frame be placed around some of

The south courtyard—an original feature that has been restored, providing daylight into the chamber.

Opposite page:
One of the new staircases built within Wallot's nineteenth-century stairwells: traces of the original stairs, removed in the 1960s rebuilding, are still visible.

Clockwise from left:
A Norman Foster sketch and detail of a newly reopened doorway in the east corridor of the Reichstag.

An example of the rediscovered graffiti written by Red Army soldiers in 1945: the old stone is distinguished from the new render by a finely incised line.

these graffiti, raising them to the level of works of art, was not approved by the Bundestag's Art Committee.

The original fabric, whether damaged by the fighting at the end of the war or by the conversion work in the 1960s, has been retained as far as possible in accordance with a concept that has been recognised since the beginning of the century, whereby conservation work should be confined to stabilising the existing fabric. Original parts of the building are clearly distinguished from those that have been added subsequently by a finely incised shadow gap marking the transitions between the two.

The Interiors

The large lobbies, corridors and bridges are restrained in mood. Glass, metal, concrete and, less frequently, stone predominate, together with the original sandstone, wherever it has survived. The floors of the corridors and foyers are paved with pale stone, offering a neutral backdrop to artworks, accents of colour, and, of course, people.

In the lobbies, the mezzanine-level bridges used by visiting members of the public are suspended and have no supporting columns. The triangular cross-section of the aluminium cladding lends these structures a slender appearance, contrasting deliberately with the heaviness of the retained stonework. The sense of hovering lightness is enhanced by the glass balustrade without intermediate posts which is used throughout the building.

The austere appearance of the newly designed public areas, with their palette of natural stone, muted greys and white, contrasts with the bright colours used elsewhere. Norman Foster was surprised when the former Chancellor Helmut Kohl, protested against the architect's original restrained concept and the Bundestag Building Committee called, in Foster's words, for "bright, welcoming, colourful interiors", especially in consideration of the younger generation of visitors.

Foster therefore worked with Danish designer Per Arnoldi to introduce more dynamic colours and the large working areas on the upper floors are designed in a much bolder style. Foster's office had already collaborated with Arnoldi on the colour design for the Frankfurt headquarters of the Commerzbank, where colour was used as a means of differentiating the various floors of the fifty-storey office tower. However, the use of colour is more problematic in a Parliament building where it might be assumed that a certain *gravitas* is required, and the effect, though generally successful, is sometimes startling.

The new conference rooms on the upper floors are lined with door-height wall panels, featuring one of twelve strong colours. They are balanced above the top of the doors by areas of plastered walling. The colours range from slate grey, through dark blue and grass green to brilliant yellow. The fact that they occasionally clash with the works of art distributed about the building is the price to pay for the warmer, more expressive colour requested by the Building Committee. Colour is also used on doorframes throughout the building to identify different floor levels and groups of activities: blue on the main parliamentary level, green on the mezzanine (tribune) level, dark red on the second-floor (presidential) level, yellow on the ground floor.

Throughout the building, certain basic dimensions recur as ordering modules. The 2.70-metre door height, for example, set the standard dimension for the wall cladding, which consists either of two 1.35-metre-high panels or three 90-centimetre-high panels arranged vertically above each other. In the latter

The west corridor at first-floor level looking north: glass, metal and stone create a neutral backdrop to art and people in the larger public areas.

The glass walls on each side of the west lobby, which create views from the west entrance right through to the chamber.

The full-height glazing behind the west portico—glass is used extensively throughout the interior.

This page, top to bottom:
The east corridor: the red doorframes indicate that this is the second-floor presidential level.

One of two stairways leading from street level to the first-floor chamber level in the eastern entrance hall.

A services access point.

Opposite page:
The east lobby at first-floor level looking north: from here there are views into the chamber from behind the eagle.

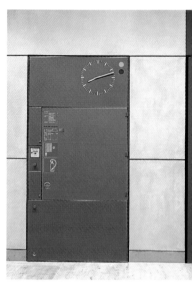

case, the middle panel frequently covers a space which contains fittings or installations: an example of this is the collection point for Members' voting cards next to the western entrance to the debating chamber.

Norman Foster and his designers also agreed the furnishings with the client. The large spaces for the political parties were furnished with cantilevered chairs designed by Mart Stam. In the smaller, more elegant rooms, such as that for the Council of Elders, Foster designed his own furnishings and fittings. Chairs and couches by well-known manufacturers such as Knoll and Cassina were also used, as were classics of modern design such as furniture by Le Corbusier, Charles Eames and Mies van der Rohe, whose 1929 Barcelona chair could scarcely be omitted. In addition to his "Kite" chair, Norman Foster was responsible for the design of the working tables. In many cases, these have leather-covered tops which weather traces of use and natural ageing well. In other cases, as in the room reserved for the use of the Chancellor, Foster designed a table with a glass top and a writing pad that can be slid aside.

Artemide lighting appears throughout the building. The large faction rooms on the third floor are daylit via glazed monopitch roofs with inbuilt screening against direct sunlight. A light-deflecting egg-crate construction between the two layers of glass permits only diffused light to enter these spaces. As everywhere in the building, additional blinds have also been installed. The brightness and the nature of the

Left:
The third-floor press lobby, which has unobstructed views down into the chamber.

lighting is controlled throughout by specially designed room control panels. These allow various lighting scenarios to be implemented, depending on the type of room and the weather conditions: for example, "house in session, sunny", "no debate, cloudy", or more prosaically "lights for cleaning operations". These panels are linked to the central management controls for the entire building.

The square corner towers accommodate smaller spaces. The tower rooms on the third floor are in use for the first time in their history to house party committee rooms. In these areas, the original bare brickwork has been left exposed and simply painted white. Curved walls tapering towards the top form a transition to the windowed tower area. The top-lights over the rooms echo the mirrored cone of the cupola with a circular glazed opening pierced by a flagpole.

Just how different Foster's treatment of the historical substance of the building is from that of the previous conversion is immediately evident in the room for the Council of Elders. Here, the existing ceiling, installed by Baumgarten, had to be retained for structural reasons. It cuts across the segmental arched windows. To ensure that the windows remain visible, the soffit is cut out in a curve at these points. Nevertheless, the spatial impression is somewhat compressed.

On the first floor of the north-east tower is the reference library. Instead

Opposite page:
A third-floor terrace with full-height shaded glazing which allows the public on the roof to see politicians circulating in the corridors below.

Below:
A third-floor faction room: there were no windows at this new level, built behind the parapet of Wallot's façades, so its rooms are daylit from above via a glazed roof.

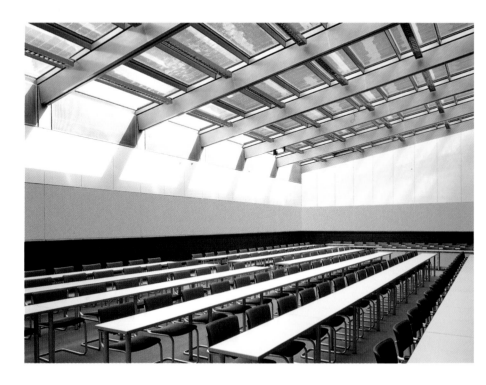

The top-light over one of the tower
rooms on the third floor, which echoes
the mirrored cone over the chamber.

Below:
A faction committee room in one
of the third-floor tower rooms: brightly
coloured panels are juxtaposed with
painted brickwork.

of wall panels, dark-blue shelf units
were built here to harmonise with
the bright red Knoll chairs. In the
Members' cafeteria, Arne Jacobsen's
stackable chairs in multiple colours
accentuate the overall colour design.
This colourful approach has been
adopted throughout the cafeterias
and dining rooms of the new
Reichstag. (The Bonn assembly hall,
dating from 1992, possesses a sim-
ilarly colourful restaurant.) The clas-
sically elegant bar on the first floor is
an extremely successful example of
how modern design can respond to
the historical proportions and even
to the grandeur of the old building
fabric without emphasizing the dif-
ferences in the stylistic approaches
of yesterday and today. In contrast
to this, the Members' restaurant on
the western side is a more neutral
space. With its large windows, it is
reminiscent of the station restau-
rants of the classic era of rail travel.

Art in the Reichstag

A total of DM 8 million was made available for the artistic embellishment of the Reichstag. At a very early date, a decision had been made to commission works by an artist from each of the four Allied nations that occupied Berlin at the end of the Second World War. The Bundestag's Art Committee regarded the new Reichstag conversion as such a genuine design achievement that they selected Norman Foster as the British representative. But that is not the whole story. The commendation was also in recognition of Foster's work in redesigning the emblematic eagle in the debating chamber.

Since 1952 an eagle designed by German sculptor Ludwig Gies, and affectionately known as the "Fat Hen", has hung in the Bonn chamber. In April 1996 Norman Foster was asked to put forward ideas for a new eagle. A number of proposals were presented but after many months of deliberation it became clear that the eagle was awakening strong political emotions. Ultimately it was decided to retain the Gies eagle but with a fundamental modification: because the Reichstag chamber has glass walls the eagle can now be seen from the back as well as the front. Foster has therefore made the eagle three-dimensional and created a new back view, which he was persuaded to sign.

Top:
American artist Jenny Holzer's digital light column in the north entrance lobby.

Opposite page:
Joseph Beuys' *Table with Aggregate* from the Bundestag's permanent collection.

French artist Christian Boltanski's installation at the entrance from the Jakob-Kaiser-House.

The eagle now works like a piece of sculpture, hovering in space.

As for the other Allied nations, to represent the United States, the experts agreed on Jenny Holzer, who installed one of her well-known digital information strips in the northern staircase. Excerpts from historic German political speeches run up the four sides of the 15-metre-high illuminated column. There are so many of them that only after a period of twenty days does the programme begin to repeat itself.

Christian Boltanski from France also took the history of the Reichstag as his theme. In the basement, directly beneath the eastern entrance to the debating chamber, is a large installation comprising 7,200 metal boxes stacked to form a chamber-like space. Each of the boxes contains the biography of a Member of Parliament; every MP who has ever sat in the democratic Parliament of Germany is represented. The records are ordered according to the dates of the Mem-

Opposite page, top to bottom:
Light boxes by Sigmar Polke in the west lobby, *Vor-Ort-Sein: Konrad Adenauer ermahnt den Fotoreporter: Jetzt haben Sie aber genug fotografiert, Kräfte-messen, Hammelsprung, Eulenspiegeleien,* and *Germania* (executed by 3D Design Köln).

Anselm Kiefer's canvas *Only with Wind, with Time and with Sound* in a first-floor committee room.

Right:
The multi-panel work, *Fundamental Lexicon*, by Grisha Bruskin in the first-floor club room.

bers' first election to Parliament. Those who were persecuted and murdered by the National Socialist regime are specially identified, revealing just how many parliament-arians paid for their work with their lives. In the middle of one wall a single black box represents the period between 1933–45 when democracy was crushed by Nazi dictatorship.

As the artistic representative of the former Soviet Union, the Committee's advisors selected Ilya Kabakov but, as described above, his suggestion to set a gold frame around some of the graffiti by Red Army soldiers was not pursued. Instead, Grisha Bruskin was commissioned to contribute a work. His piece, *Fundamental Lexicon*, comprises a number of panels showing historical characters from Peter the Great to the soldier who raised the Red Flag over the Reichstag, and this work adorns one wall of the first-floor club room.

The choice of German artists was controversial, as was only to be expected. The Art Committee set a high standard with the concept it put forward in October 1997. Underlining the special nature of the Reichstag building and its "eventful history, which is so rich in references to the fate of the German people", the Committee recommended "mainly German artists of international fame and in particular from the former German Democratic Republic". Commissions were to be

81

awarded "especially to those who have occupied themselves primarily with the subjects of German politics and society or who have had a significant influence in these areas".

A number of artists from the former East Germany have a stronger relationship to politics and especially to history than their colleagues from West Germany. Among the East German artists chosen was Bernhard Heisig, a prominent representative of the figurative Leipzig School. His panorama of German history, *Time and Life* in the small cafeteria on the first floor has conscious echoes of the Socialist Realist art that predominated in the old GDR. Works by representatives of more dissident artistic movements from the former East were also acquired.

The most acclaimed artists from the former West Germany were also nominated. In the western entrance hall are works by Sigmar Polke and Gerhard Richter. Polke is represented with five visual puzzles based on German myths; Richter with a 22-metre-high variation of the German flag comprising six monochrome glass panels arranged to form a horizontally banded flag. Georg Baselitz contributed two paraphrases of woodcuts by Caspar David Friedrich, which hang in the staircase in the southern entrance.

There are also works by Gotthard Graubner, Karl-Georg Pfahler, Hanne Darboven, Rosemarie Trockel and others. These are situated in the committee and conference rooms on the upper floors. Ulrich Rückriem was able to realise a floor sculpture in the southern courtyard that affirms the artist's insistence on the autonomy of his work.

The multi-denominational devotional space for the Reichstag presented a particular challenge. Günther Uecker is best known for his distinctive use of nails and he has used these here to great effect. He has worked in close collaboration with the architects to create a simple space for quiet contemplation.

As early as 1992, prior to the conversion, Katharina Sieverding's work commemorating the Members of the Reichstag who had been persecuted and murdered by the National Socialists was installed in the Reichstag; it graced the hall from whose balcony Philipp Scheidemann had proclaimed the Republic on 9 November 1918. This five-part photographic work has now been located in the corresponding space on the south side of the building which serves as a lobby for the

Left:
Günther Uecker's multi-faith chapel on the first floor.

Members of the Bundestag. The Scheidemann Room is now the Members' restaurant and contains a fresco by Markus Lüpertz.

Further works of art were purchased after these commissions had been awarded. A decision was made not to retain other works from the period of the earlier conversion of the Reichstag building.

Above:
Katharina Sieverding's memorial to persecuted members of the Reichstag in the first-floor Members' lobby.

Following page:
The view from the west lobby into the chamber: the podium has been restored to its original position in the east so that it is immediately visible to visitors climbing the west stairs.

The Debating Chamber

Within the building, the debating chamber provides the outstanding spatial experience. The hall is situated on the first-floor level, or *piano nobile*. The floor of the chamber is sunk by up to 1.40 metres below this level to provide the necessary incline for the rows of seating.

A number of elements combine to make this space particularly impressive: its great breadth, its equally impressive height, the large areas of glazing that admit daylight from all sides, and the sense of weightlessness created at the heart of such a massive building. Foster's intention was that the plenary chamber

Below:
The view from behind the eagle in the east lobby shows the strong sense of transparency in the chamber.

should be at the heart of the rebuilt Reichstag and should be light, open and visually and publicly accessible.

Foster recalls: "Originally the Reichstag was compartmentalised and highly stratified. We have gouged through these layers from top to bottom, opening up the building to light and views."

Twelve slender spun-concrete columns support the outer ring of the roof, from which an equal number of tapering beams cantilever out to bear the load of the inner ring. This in turn supports the mirrored cone. These columns are visually elegant, and slender in diameter, and they mediate visually between the circular shape of the chamber and the rectangular form of the building, which remains visible through the side windows to the two courtyards and the fully glazed walls of the eastern and western entrance halls.

Chambers of this kind are acoustically problematic if they do not have some kind of sound-absorbing surfaces. As we know from earlier parliaments, the speaking voice needs the help of technology. Speeches are relayed by more than 200 microphones and 300 loud-speakers distributed around the hall

so that every speaker is clearly audible from everwhere in the chamber.

Anyone who recalls the lengthy wrangling over the arrangement of the seating for the new parliamentary chamber in Bonn by Günter Behnisch, may well be surprised at the arrangement of the debating chamber in Berlin, where the layout seems so logical. Democracy in a Parliament with more than two opposed parties requires a circular arrangement to reflect different electoral results and party strengths. The seating for the 669 Members of the Bundestag is arranged in an ellipse, rising in steps from front to back. Cut into the ellipse and facing it in a segmental curve are the benches for Members of the cabinet and the Bundesrat. The legislature and the elected executive are, therefore, seated facing each other. This is a compromise between the old Waterworks in Bonn—where the Bundestag was based until 1992— and Behnisch's chamber, where everyone was seated democratically in a true circle, a solution that was considered not to be entirely successful.

Left:
The light cone seen from the third-floor press lobby.

The colouring of the debating chamber is somewhat spartan. The grey of the exposed concrete is complemented by the silvery shimmering metal elements and by a diffuse brightness resulting from the large areas of glass. The almost 8-metre-high federal eagle—now in aluminium—also gleams in a restrained grey tone. The only note of colour is provided by the seating in "Reichstag blue", as it was quickly nicknamed. This seems to oscillate in tone between ultramarine and violet, depending on lighting conditions. The pale timber of the Speaker's rostrum and the tiers of seating for the Bundestag presidential team scarcely strikes a contrast. The six tribunes, each with 73 seats, upholstered in grey fabric, are also restrained in colour.

These tribunes project far into the chamber above the rear rows of Members' seats, and were designed to draw the 400 (maximum) visitors into the centre of events, close to the Speaker's rostrum and the nearby seats for the cabinet and party leaders. As a result, the considerable size of the chamber, with an area of 1,200 square metres, appears quite intimate.

The Roof Terrace and Cupola

The roof is the public domain. Like the western entrance with its foyer extending the full height of the building, the roof terrace and cupola are immediately accessible to the general public at all times, whereas the debating chamber is open only to visitors who have made arrangements in advance.

The concept of transparency that has dominated discussions about parliamentary buildings in Germany for decades is captured by the cupola in a surprising, innovative and entirely direct manner. Here Foster was able not only to make functional use of the principle of transparency, but also to create a powerful symbol. By day, when visitors are sketchily visible on the double helix of the ramps, but even more so at night, when the glazed structure shines like a beacon, the cupola is a sign, in the best sense of the word. It signals the presence of the debating chamber immediately below in a form that is recognizable from afar as a striking feature on the urban skyline.

The cupola has a diameter of 40 metres at its base and rises to a height of 23.5 metres, far above the roofs of the surrounding buildings. The structure consists of 24 curved steel ribs that support a steel ring at the top. Horizontally, the cupola is braced by 17 steel rings. At the top is a tension ring with a circular opening 8 metres in diameter. The steel structure has a total weight of 800 tonnes. The cupola is clad with roughly 3,000 square metres of glass fixed in a scale-like manner in a series of angled tiers. At intervals the horizontal glazing between facets is omitted to permit the circulation of air. Otherwise, the spaces between the layers are closed by strips of glass angled to correspond with the inclination of the more than 400 glass "scales".

The glazing allows visitors on the 230-metre-long spiralling ramps an

Left:
Photovoltaic panels on the south-facing side of the roof which convert sunlight into electricity to drive the sun-shade in the cupola.

Opposite page:
The great public roof terrace which leads to the entry points to the glass cupola.

unimpeded view over Berlin. The double ramp has a gradient of eight degrees and is suspended by steel tension members from the 24 structural ribs. People ascending the ramps to the viewing platform at the top cannot actually see down into the chamber except at night or when television lights are in use. (By comparison, the press lobby at third-floor level has uninterrupted views into the chamber). But the MPs can see the visitors—a reminder that there are people out there whom they represent.

Set within the lantern is the "light sculptor", a concave mirrored cone with 360 angled mirrors that reflect daylight downwards into the depths of the chamber. The cone is 15 metres in diameter at its top at public viewing platform level, and 2.5 metres at the point where it pierces

the chamber ceiling. At this point it is held in position by slender steel "bicycle-wheel" spokes before tapering to point over the chamber. Within the cupola, a sun-shade powered by photovoltaic cells on the roof tracks the path of the sun to prevent problems of solar heat and glare in the chamber while allowing a little sunlight to play on the chamber floor. The diffused daylight that this creates is quite adequate to light the chamber. In fact, the system brings light so effectively into the chamber that electric lighting is needed only on the gloomiest of days.

Possibly it was the glazed form of the structure that reconciled Foster with the client's request for a dome. It sits so lightly on the massive building that it could not be mistaken for a reproduction of the heavy former

structure nor for a genuflection to Wallot. Housed in an inconspicuous structure on the eastern side of the roof is a public restaurant, which promises to become a permanent attraction because of its breath-taking views, especially in the evening. This, too, is an act of respect towards the ultimate authority in a democratic state, the people.

Above:
The outside terrace of the rooftop
restaurant which offers spectacular
views of Berlin.

Left:
The rooftop restaurant, where MPs and
the public can dine together.

Following pages:
The concave mirrored cone of the "light
sculptor" inside the cupola: its 360 angled
mirrors reflect daylight deep into the
chamber.

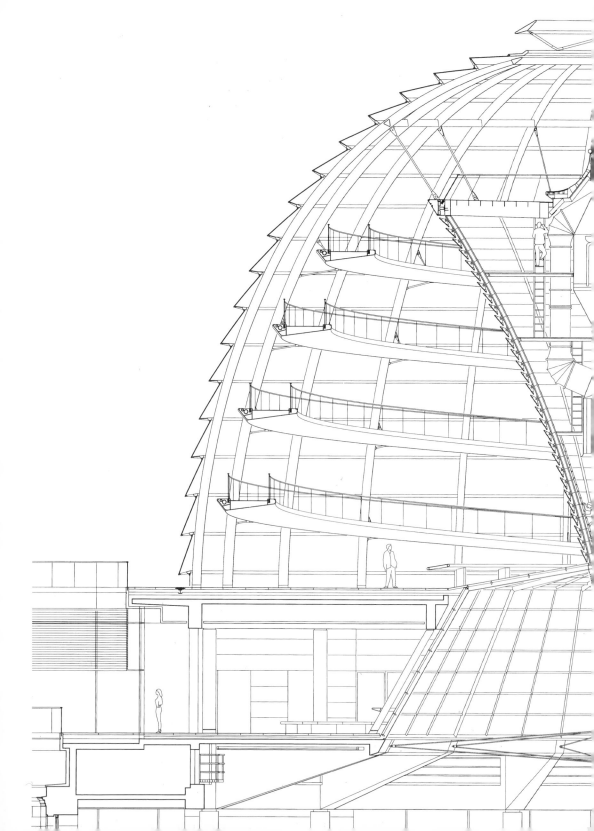

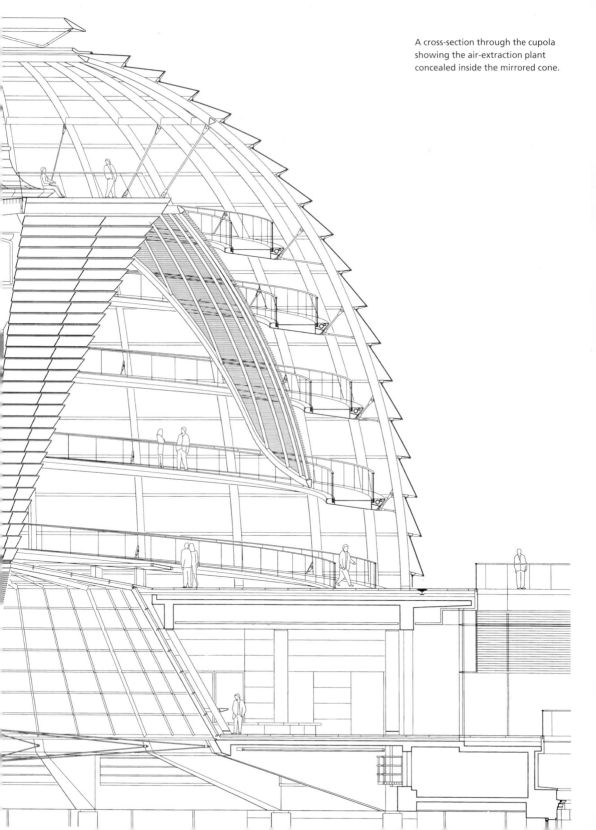

A cross-section through the cupola
showing the air-extraction plant
concealed inside the mirrored cone.

Above:
The opening at the top of the cupola
with its aerodynamic "spoiler", which
encourages air-flow.

Previous page:
Members of the public ascending the
spiral ramps to the observation platform
at the top of the cupola. In the left fore-
ground is the moveable sun-shade.

Right:
The vent at the top of the cone, where
exhaust air from the chamber is emitted.

The Energy Concept

From the outset, Norman Foster attached the utmost importance to implementing a forward-looking energy concept as part of the conversion programme for the Reichstag. The original design of a huge canopy over the building was justified by the advantages it would bring in terms of daylighting and ventilation. A different solution had to be found for the conversion scheme that was finally executed, however.

The design of the cupola grew in part from its daylighting function, as described earlier. But the cupola is just one part of a comprehensive and innovative energy concept that includes both the generation of energy, in the form of heat and electricity, and its reduced consumption. In its own home, the Bundestag wanted to set an example of ecological awareness. Savings have been made especially in the area of heating and cooling, where there has been such an appalling waste of energy in many office buildings in the past. In the future, the electricity requirements for the entire parliamentary area are to be supplied by two decentralised district heating and power plants. One is situated in the basement of the north-eastern tower of the Reichstag building.

Only when all the buildings to be served by this system have been completed and linked up will it be possible to judge the success of the energy concept of the technical co-operative for the parliamentary buildings (TVP). The goals are ambitious. A combined heat and power

generator burns vegetable oil from rape or sunflower seeds, also known as bio-diesel. When burned in a co-generator to produce electricity, bio-diesel is extremely efficient and it should be possible to reduce the emission of carbon dioxide to 440 tonnes a year. Foster notes that the energy balance of the Reichstag building after its previous conversion in the 1960s showed an emission of 7,000 tonnes of carbon dioxide a year. The co-generating plants are de-

Combined Heat and Power Plant

Absorption Cooling Plant

Heat Pump

Electrical Power

Heating

Refined Vegetable Oil

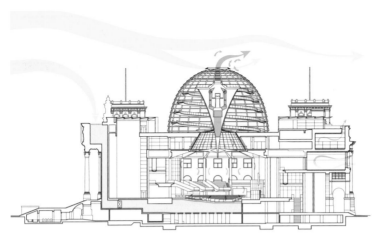

signed to cover 80 per cent of the electrical needs and more than 90 per cent of the heating needs of the parliamentary area through the combined generation of heat and power (using waste heat from the generation of electricity). The Berlin power supply system will be used only as a back-up system for the area as a whole, but is not required at all for the Reichstag.

Surplus heat generated by the power plant will be used to regulate the internal climate of the Reichstag and, at a later date, some of the surrounding office buildings.

Below the building are two aquifer reservoirs. Surplus heat is discharged as warm water down one of two boreholes into the deeper of these reservoirs, 300 metres beneath the Reichstag, where it can be stored with practically no drop in temperature. In winter it can be pumped back via the second borehole to the surface again to heat the building via under-floor pipes. It can also be fed through an absorption cooling unit which produces chilled water. This in turn can be stored in a second aquifer reservoir situated at a depth of roughly 60 metres which contains cold water at a temperature of approximately 5 °C. In summer, the cold water will be employed in a similar way to absorb heat and cool the building via chilled ceilings.

The cupola represents the most important element in the energy concept. Its function in daylighting the chamber has been described above. The exploitation of natural light is reflected in the energy balance by a clearly reduced consumption of electricity which would otherwise be necessary for artificial lighting. But the cupola also serves to ventilate the debating chamber via a ventilation system housed within the mirrored cone.

Fresh air is drawn into the building above the western portico; the prevailing winds in Berlin are from the west and bring cool, fresh air from the Tiergarten district. The air

The maintenance hatchway in the open position at the top of the cone.

The grille at the top of the chamber which draws out naturally rising hot air and expels it from the top of the cone.

forgotten in modern architecture.

The air ducts now being used in the Reichstag building are the ones installed in the original building. With the assistance of the American engineer David Grove, Wallot incorporated a naturally functioning ventilation system, the basis of which bore a striking resemblance to the present installation.

The great thermal mass of the Wallot building also provides a passive form of temperature control. The great thickness of the walls (up to 2 metres) means that the building responds only slowly to temperature changes. While this can be a problem, meaning that the building can take a long time to warm up in winter, it is also a blessing because the building keeps out a lot of heat in summer. Foster has optimised such natural energy-saving devices with a combination of state-of-the-art technology and sound traditional techniques.

The Reichstag energy concept is complemented by a photovoltaic installation on the south-facing section of the roof which has a peak output of approximately 40 kW. As well as driving the sun-shade in the cupola this powers mechanical fans within the cone that assist the ventilation process when required. Heat exchangers make it possible to recover and utilise a proportion of the heat from the extract air before it is expelled through the top of the cupola.

For a long time now, especially in Germany, great importance has been attached in new buildings to the use of natural ventilation sys-

tems allowing individual temperature control. However, these have the drawback of allowing in noise and hot sunlight, as well as being a security risk. The windows designed for the Reichstag therefore use the original openings fitted with a system of intelligent windows with two layers of glass which balance out extreme fluctuations of temperature. The inner window can be opened from the inside either manually or automatically. The outer layer is laminated with a protective coating and has ventilation joints which admit air from the outside. The void between houses a solar shading device.

intake is conducted via large ducts into a plenum beneath the debating chamber, from where it enters the chamber through perforated mesh in the floor and the loose-weave carpet which acts as a filter. Warmed by various heat sources, such as lighting and the people in the chamber, the air rises to the ceiling, where it is drawn into the funnel-shaped cone through grilles in the sides. Waste air is emitted at the top of the cone and escapes through the eight-metre-diameter opening in the cupola. The lantern opening is fitted with a wind spoiler to encourage air flow across the top of the cupola and facilitate the extraction process.

The system is based on the traditional solar chimney and the natural rising of the heated air, encouraged by the "flue" effect of the cone and cupola, is sufficient to maintain the whole process of air circulation. Only with the advent of energy-intensive mechanical ventilation plant was this naturally generated system

Below:
The plenum beneath the chamber: fresh air is channeled here after it is drawn in above the west portico via ducts which date from Wallot's time.

A view of the Reichstag and east Berlin
from the Tiergarten, one of the "lungs"
of the city.

The Reichstag in the German Capital

The Parliamentary and Government District

The strangely unreal appearance of the Reichstag hitherto was largely attributable to its out-of-the-way position. Its state of isolation within the city is now drawing to an end. In the future, the building will form the centre of the entire parliamentary district and one of the two dominant structures in the capital, together with the new Chancellery situated at the opposite, western, end of the Spreebogen. The decision to integrate the Spreebogen, the area formed by the great curve in the River Spree at this point, into the political functions of the capital formed the basis for the urban planning competition held in 1992–93.

This decision dates back to earlier resolutions made in the 1950s, however, when the area had been allocated as the quarter for a future capital of a united Germany, and it has been kept free of development since then. It took a stroke of genius

on the part of Axel Schultes, who proposed a "Federal Strip" stretching along the Spree and crossing it in two places, to define and clarify the relationship between the Reichstag and its surroundings.

The concept behind this federal mile was to group the most important buildings in the capital in such a way that they would form a unit; secondly, the proposals sought to tie the two parts of Berlin—East and West—together. The Reichstag itself does not form part of the federal mile: but the strip is clearly related to the building. More than 1.5 kilometres long and at least 100 metres wide, the "Federal Strip" runs parallel to the north face of the Reichstag.

The most important building and, having undergone the requisite modifications, the most physically outstanding structure actually within the strip, is the Chancellor's office. Located in its immediate vicinity are the offices and committee buildings of the German Bundestag. The Munich architect Stephan Braunfels succeeded in giving this development a memorable form with a design on a par with the urban planning concept.

Other offices are being built on sites to the east of the Reichstag on both sides of the Dorotheenstrasse. Five architectural practices have been brought together for this purpose with each office designing its own section of the development independently of the others, yet in compliance with the overall concept and constraints of conservation. The variations between the individual buildings and their façades are intended to indicate the former pattern of site divisions along this historical street, even if these no longer exist.

Although the buildings along the Dorotheenstrasse observe the scale of the other developments in this central district of Berlin, in the spirit of a "critical reconstruction", Stephan Braunfels was also able to address the new and, for Berlin, unusual form of Schultes' Federal Strip in his development to the north of the Reichstag. Braunfels' proposals to accommodate the spatial programme for his scheme in two buildings on the far side of the River Spree represent the first step in translating the urban planning concept into architecture. The idea of locating the Bundestag library, the third-largest parliamentary library in the world, in a cylinder integrated into the overall built structure on the other side of the river underlines the need to make this leap across the Spree, to link the two parts of the development on opposite sides of the river.

At one time, the library was housed in the eastern part of the Reichstag building itself on intermediate floors that were not legible on the outside. During the 1920s, a new location had been sought for the library directly opposite the north side of the building between the Reichstag and the river, but the various architectural competitions that were held were never put into effect, and finally the demise of the Weimar Republic put an end to all lofty plans of this nature. On 1 May 1945, the irreplaceable contents of this library were destroyed by fire in a store in the centre of Berlin where they had been placed for safe keeping. They thus fell victim to the confusion accompanying the final stage of hostilities at the end of the Second World War.

Now, for the first time in its history, the Reichstag will be a fully functioning building in an efficient parliamentary district. To the east the new buildings in the Dorotheenstrasse form a link with the old city centre; the Reichstag's south façade overlooks a corner of the Tiergarten, as it always has; and the west façade towers over the Platz der Republik, where the citizens of Berlin have historically demonstrated their will for freedom, most notably in 1948 in protest against the Soviet Blockade.

The former Congress Hall is situated in what is a continuation of the square. The hall was a gift donated by the United States to West Berlin on the occasion of the International Building Exhibition held in 1957. Today, the hall accommodates the House of the Cultures of the World. The varied activities held there demonstrate just how international Berlin's population has long been, and also how irreversibly liberal-minded and cosmopolitan the policies of the Berlin Republic have to remain.

A view of the cupola from the Brandenburg Gate: the new Parliament of the reunified Germany is situated on the former frontline between East and West.

The Reichstag as a Symbol of German Unity

The self-portrayal of the Federal Republic of Germany through its architecture has been the subject of criticism from many quarters recently. Since a historical stroke of fate, German reunification, brought the post-war era to an end, the old Federal Republic has fallen into disrepute because of its forgetfulness of its own history. The architectural expression the nation found in Bonn, its eternally provisional capital, and in innumerable public buildings elsewhere suddenly seemed too puny, too inconsequential and unconsidered for the unusual political role and responsibility the German state had assumed. On the other hand, the record of the past preserved in the ruins of Berlin frightened those who wanted a new beginning for Germany without the burden of history. Often enough, the aversion towards Berlin becoming the capital was underpinned with images of the city's architecture and the role it had played in the past.

In the meantime, looking back on a decade of unification, of which the late Willy Brandt, the former Chancellor and ex-Mayor of Berlin, spoke in the historic month of November 1989, all this may be regarded as a passing phenomenon accompanying the profound process of transformation which the state and society are undergoing. The Reichstag building reflects this process in its own way. It is, incidentally, not the only former seat of Parliament in Berlin that is being used again by an appropriate public body: the former Prussian Landtag building has been occupied since 1994 by the House of Representatives of the state of Berlin; and the Bundesrat—the federal council or upper chamber of the German Parliament—which took a long time to make up its mind to move to Berlin, is taking up residence in the former upper chamber of the Prussian Parliament. In terms of their architectural and historical importance, neither of these two houses can be compared with the Reichstag. Nevertheless, it is worth noting that they are not encumbered by the past, and they are both open to a new and evolving tradition of public institutions within a democratic state.

Nowhere is this reconciliation of past and present expressed more clearly than in the converted Reichstag building. In its juxtaposition of respect for history and bold innovation, the design by Norman Foster shows that it is possible, indeed right, to link the past with the present without having to resort to pastiche. It need not concern us that the symbolic cupola, for example, was the outcome of a long quest for an acceptable compromise, a quest that took a number of surprising turns. Compromise is an attribute of democracy. Given the symbolic character of the Reichstag, the acceptance of its historical content in combination with the risks inherent in a modern new design represents a compromise in the best sense of the word.

The end of the much-invoked "special German path" has finally been reached; at this point, it merges with the broad avenue of classical Western democracy. This is one way in which the symbolic meaning of the Reichstag can be related to the course of post-war German history. If the message of the newly designed building is understood in this way, then Foster's work has found its just place at the centre of the capital of the Federal Republic of Germany.

Following page:
The new glass cupola is a powerful symbol of renewal and democracy, visible for miles around.

Norman Foster

Norman Foster was born in Manchester, England, in 1935. After graduating from Manchester University School of Architecture and City Planning in 1961, he won a Fellowship to Yale University where he gained a Master's Degree in Architecture.

Foster Associates was founded in 1967 and is now known as Foster and Partners. Since its inception the practice has received more than190 awards and citations for excellence and has won 50 national and international competitions.

Major buildings include: Willis Faber & Dumas Head Office, Ipswich, 1975; Sainsbury Centre for Visual Arts , Norwich, 1978; Hongkong and Shanghai Bank, Hong Kong, 1985; Sackler Galleries at the Royal Academy, London, 1991; Stansted, London's Third International Airport, 1991; Century Tower in Tokyo, 1991; Carré d'Art, Nîmes, 1993; Commerzbank Headquarters, Frankfurt, 1997; American Air Museum, Duxford, 1997; and the new Hong Kong International Airport at Chek Lap Kok, 1998.

Recent projects include the Great Court of the British Museum and the new Millennium Bridge, London.

Norman Foster was awarded the RIBA Royal Gold Medal for Architecture in 1983, the Gold Medal of the French Academy of Architecture in 1991 and the AIA Gold Medal in 1994. He was appointed Officer of the Order of the Arts and Letters from the Ministry of Culture in France also in 1994. In 1990 he was granted a Knighthood in the Queen's Birthday Honours and appointed by the Queen to the Order of Merit in 1997. In 1999 he became the 21st Pritzker Architecture Prize Laureate and in the same year he was also honoured with a Life Peerage in the Queen's Birthday Honours List, taking the title Lord Foster of Thames Bank.

Bibliography

Architektenverein zu Berlin/ Vereinigung Berliner Architekten (ed.): *Berlin und seine Bauten*, Bd. II/III, Der Hochbau, Berlin 1896 (reprint Berlin 1988), pp. 53–65

Baal-Teshuva, Jacob (ed.): *Christo: The Reichstag and Urban Projects*, Munich 1993

Baumeister, No. 6/1999 (special Reichstag issue): Umbau des Reichstags in Berlin

Bauwelt, No. 18/19, 14.5.1999 (special Reichstag issue): *Der Bundestag im Herzen von Berlin*

Berlin Information Centre: *Outlook Berlin*, Berlin 1985

Borchardt, Claire: *Die Konstruktion der Reichstagskuppel*, in: Düttmann, Martina/Zwoch, Felix (ed.): *Bauwelt Berlin Annual 1997*, Basle, Berlin, Boston 1998, pp. 26–31

Buddensieg, Tilmann: *Das Reichstagsgebäude von Paul Wallot. Rätsel und Antworten seiner Formensprache*, in: Wefing, pp. 30–43

Bundesbaudirektion Berlin (ed.): *Realisierungswettbewerb Umbau Reichstagsgebäude zum Deutschen Bundestag (Ausschreibung)*, 2 vols., Berlin 1992

Bundesbaudirektion Berlin (ed.): *Realisierungswettbewerb Umbau des Reichstagsgebäudes zum Deutschen Bundestag (Ergebnisse)*, Berlin 1993

Bundesbaugesellschaft Berlin (ed.): *Schlüsselübergabe Reichstagsgebäude: Der Umbau zum Sitz des Deutschen Bundestages ist vollendet*, Berlin 1999

see also: *Berliner Morgenpost*: supplement for the edition of 18.4.1999

Berliner Zeitung: Der Reichstag, supplement for the edition of 17./18.4.1999

Der Tagesspiegel: Der Bundestag im Reichstag, supplement for the edition of 19.4.1999

Cullen, Michael S.: *Der Reichstag. Geschichte eines Monumentes*, Berlin 1983

Cullen, Michael S.: *Der Reichstag Parlament, Denkmal, Symbol*, Berlin 1995

Cullen, Michael S./Kieling, Uwe: *Der Deutsche Reichstag. Geschichte eines Parlaments*, Berlin 1992

Deutscher Bundestag: *The Reichstag: Scene of German Parliamentary History*, Bonn 1985

Dieckmann, Friedrich: *Preiswürdige Irrwege. Die Ergebnisse des Reichstagswettbewerbs*, in: Dieckmann, Friedrich: *Wege durch Mitte. tadterfahrungen*, Berlin 1995

Foster, Norman: *New German Parliament, Reichstag Berlin*, in: Foster, Norman: *Selected and Current Works of Foster and Partners*, Mulgrave 1992, pp. 162–167

Foster, Norman: *Ein optimistisches' Zeichen für ein modernes Deutschland. Über den Umbau des Berliner Reichstagsgebäudes*, in: Wefing, pp. 180–191

Foster, Norman: *Rebuilding the Reichstag*, London 2000

Mönninger, Michael: *Rückkehr in die Hauptstadt. Politik und Architektur in Berlin*, in: Berliner Festspiele/

Architektenkammer Berlin (ed.): *Berlin: Offene Stadt. Die Erneuerung seit 1989*, Berlin 1999, pp. 38–53

Pritchard, John: *Reichstag Fire – Ashes of Democracy*, New York 1972

Raack, Heinz: *Das Reichstagsgebäude in Berlin*, Berlin 1978

Schmädeke, Jürgen: *Der Deutsche Reichstag. Geschichte und Gegenwart eines Bauwerks*, Erweiterte Neuausgabe, Munich 1994

Süssmuth, Rita, President of the German Bundestag (ed.): *Kolloquium Reichstag. Berichte, Hintergründe, Bilder*, Bonn 1992

see also: Deutscher Bundestag: *Kolloquium Reichstag. Stenographischer Bericht*, Bonn 1992

Wefing, Heinrich (ed.): *"Dem Deutschen Volke". Der Bundestag im Berliner Reichstagsgebäude*, Bonn 1999

Welch Guerra, Max: *Hauptstadt Einig Vaterland. Planung und Politik zwischen Bonn und Berlin*, Berlin 1999

Wise, Michael Z.: Norman Foster's Reichstag: *Illuminating Shadows of the Past*, in: Wise, Michael Z.: *Capital Dilemma. Germany's Search for a New Architecture of Democracy*, New York 1998, pp. 121–134

Facts and Figures

Cost: DM 600 million

Total area: 61,166 square metres

Net area: 11,200 square metres

Length: 137.4 metres

Width: 93.9 metres

Height: 47 metres

Number of storeys: 6 + Dome

Competition first stage: 1992

Competition second stage: 1993

Construction begun: July 1995

Topping out ceremony:
   18 September 1997

Official opening: 19 April 1999

Workforce and Construction

More than 25 trade contractors.

240 workers on site each day
   during demolition.

Up to 46 people in Fosters' Berlin
   office.

1100 drawings were submitted, presented in 65 folders.

45,000 tonnes of demolition material removed from the central area of the chamber, in 35 truckloads per day from October 1995 to February 1996, using a caterpillar machine with a 43-metre boom. Altogether, one third of the fabric removed.

12 fairfaced spun-concrete columns in the chamber, each weighing 23 tonnes, carry the load of the dome.

Light Sculptor (Cone)

Weight: 300 tonnes

2.5 metres across at its base, where it punctures the chamber ceiling, widening to 16 metres.

The new cupola: symbolism and functionalism are integrated in a major feat of engineering.

Covered with 360 highly reflective glass mirrors.

Computerised sun-tracking movable shield powered by photovoltaic cells prevents penetration of solar heat and glare.

Cupola

Height: 23.5 metres

Diameter: 40 metres

Total weight: 1200 tonnes

Weight of steel: 800 tonnes

Clad in 3000 square metres of laminated safety glass—two layers of glass with an intermediate layer of vinyl foil—panel size 5.10 m x 1.80 m max.

1.6 metre-wide helical ramps integral to structure of cupola, providing lateral stiffening and vertical loading.

Observation platform height: 40.7 metres

Ecological Features

Natural ventilation in the chamber using fresh air drawn up by the flue effect of the cone and cupola.

Heat exchangers recover and reutilise warm air not expelled through the cupola.

"Intelligent windows" comprise manually operated inner layer and security-laminated outer layer which draws in fresh air via ventilation joints.

Renewable vegetable bio-fuel burned in a co-generator produces clean electricity, reducing annual carbon dioxide output by 94 per cent.

Surplus heat stored in natural aquifer 300 metres below ground which provides hot water for heating.

Cold water is stored in an aquifer 60 metres below ground to provide cooling via chilled ceilings in hot weather.

Photovoltaic cells cover 300 square metres on south roof.

General

Approximately 750 seats, one for every MP, arranged according to respective party groupings.

Rooftop restaurant for MPs, press and members of the public.

Press room and bar in ambulatory around the glazed soffit of the chamber, with views of parliamentary proceedings.

Foster and Partners
Project Team

Norman Foster
David Nelson
Mark Braun
Stefan Behling
Ulrich Hamann
Christian Hallmann
Dieter Muller
Ingo Pott

Christofer Allerkamp
Claudia Ayaz
Nick Baker
John Ball
Tanya von Barnau
Alexander Barry
Stephan Baumgart
Simon Beames
Serge Belet
Susanne Bellinghausen
Nicola Bielski
Toby Blunt
Etienne Borgos
Giuseppe Boscherini
Simon Bowden
Arthur Branthwaite
George Brennan
Caroline Brown
Hing Chan
Kei-Lu Cheong
Rachel Clark
Charles Collett
Mark-Andrew Costello
Brian Thomas Ditchburn
Ilona Dohn
Ivo Dolezalek
Robert Dörr
John Drew
Constance Edwards
Benjamin Ellwanger
Matteo Fantoni
Henri Louis Ferretti
Anja Flesch
Mark Ford
Kevin Galvin
Susanne Geiger
Xenia Genth
Martin Geyer
Russell Gilchrist
Frank Glaesener
Ulrich Goertz
Helen Goodland
Niall Greenan
Nigel Greenhill

Tanya Griffiths
Daniela Grijakovic
Adelheid Gross
Pedro Haberbosch
Brandon Haw
Andreas Hell
Oliver Hempel
Anne Hengst
Wendelin Hinsch
Robert Hoh
Alison Holroyd
Wiliam Hunt
Ken Hutt
Martin Hyams
Thomas Ibach
Helmut Jacoby
Nadi Jahangiri
Michael Jakob
Adrienne Johnson
Rebecca Jones
Ralph Klabunde
Dirk Koslowski
Carsten Krohn
Madeline Lee
Ian Lomas
Ellen van Loon
Andrea Ludwig
Valérie Lutton-Laub
Alan Marten-Wilkinson
Giles Martin
David McDowell
Emma McHugh
Michelle Meier
Rudi Meisel
Olaf Menk
Andreas Mertens
Jons Messedat
Julia Mooney
Max Neal
Uwe Nienstedt
Matthew Parker
Sunil Parmar
Robin Partington
Simon Peckham
Nikki Pipe
Andrea Platena
Tony Price
Adam Pritchard
Dagmar Quentin
Michael Richter
Tilman Richter von Senfft
Jan Roth
Matthias Rudolph

Sans Ruiz Montserrat
Gudrun Sack
John de Salvo
Peer Schärer
Robert Schmid
Paul Scott
Wei Y Seah
Rupert Sherwood
Ken Shuttleworth
John Small
Paul Sommer
Kinna Stallard
Kai Strehl
Henning Stummel
Mark Sutcliffe
Bernd Treide
Huw Turner
Ruggero Venelli
Juan Vieria
Wilhelm Vossenkuhl
Ken Wai
Robert Watson
Antoine Weygand
Rolf Wiethege
Joh. Michael Zeuner

Presentation Drawings
Andrew Birds, Richard Portchmouth,
Michael Russum, John Hewitt,
Ted Nielan, Michail Blösser

Client
Federal Republic of Germany
represented by Bundesbaugesellschaft Berlin mbH

Consultants

Acoustics
IKP, Professor Dr Georg Plenge
Müller BBM GmbH

Catering Facilities
LZ Plan-Team

Cladding Consultants
Emmer Pfenninger Partner AG

Conservation Consultants
Acanthus

Fire Protection
Professor W Klingsch

**Lifts, Materials, Handling
Technology**
Jappsen & Stangier

Lighting
Claude and Danielle Engle

**Mechanical, Electrical and
Services**
Amstein & Walthert
Fischer Energie and Haustechnik
Kaiser Bautechnik
Kuehn Associates
Planungsgruppe Karnasch-Hackstein

Project Management
ARGE Projektsteuerung Reichstag,
Professor Weiß & Partner
and Weidleplan

Quantity Surveyors
Davis Langdon & Everest

Quantity Surveyor, Site Supervision
Büro Am Lützowplatz

Structural Engineer
Leonhardt Andrä & Partner
Ove Arup & Partners
Schlaich Bergermann & Partner

Suppliers and Subcontractors

Acoustic Blinds
Clauss Markiesen GmbH

Alarm Systems
BOSCH TELECOM Leipzig GmbH,
Telenorma VN Berlin

Asbestos Removal
ARGE Reichstag Berlin-Asbest,
E. Schütze GmbH, HAKAP-Berlin
GmbH

Carpets
Anker Teppichfabrik,
Gebrüder Scholler GmbH + Co KG

Chairs
Howe A/S, Tecno SA,
Gebrüder Thonet GmbH, Walter Knoll,
Vitra GmbH

Core and Shell
ARGE Hochbau Reichstag,
Ed. Züblin AG,
Dechant Bau GmbH,
Löhn Hochbau

Demolition
ARGE Rückbau Reichstag,
Ingenieur- und Tiefbau Gmb

Door Handles
Valli & Valli Fusital

Dome Construction and Cladding
ARGE Reichstagskuppel,
Waagner-Biro GmbH Wien

Electrical Systems and Wiring
Elektro-Anlagenbau Wismar GmbH

Facades and Windows
ARGE Götz GmbH/Dillingen,
Waagner-Biro GmbH München/Wien

Fireproofing
Svt Brandschutz GmbH, Total Walther

Fit Out—Ceilings, Render, Dry Walls
Klaus Rogge GmbH, Spezialtiefbau

Fit Out—Chamber
Lindner AG

Fit Out—Counters
Ostfriesische Möbelwerkstätten

**Fit Out—Wall Panels, Doors,
Built-in Elements**
Vereinigte Holzbaubetriebe,
W.Pfalzer und H.

Furniture
Artemide, Cassina SpA,
Fritz Hausen A/S, Knoll International,
Tecno SA, Wilkhahm GmbH & Co

Glass Panels
BGT Bischoff Glastechnik
GmbH & Co KG

Glass Walls and Doors (Internal)
Magnus Müller GmbH & Co KG

Kitchen Equipment
ARGE Elektrolux Professional GmbH,
Therma Großküchen GmbH
ARGE (Großküchentechnische
Einrichtungen),
Therma Großküchen

Lifts
Fujitec, Deutschland GmbH

Lighting—Dome, Wall Washing
BEGA, Gantenbrink Leuchten
GmbH + Co.

Lighting—Interiors
ERCO Leuchten GmbH

Locks and Keys
Weckbacher GmbH

Maintenance and Cleaning Systems
Greifzug GmbH

**M+E—Heat Storage Drilling and
Planning**
BLM Gesellschaft für Bohrlochphysik
und geoökologische Messungen
mbH, E+M, Bohr-und Brunnenbau
GmbH

Metalwork
Kirchgässner E-Technik GmbH,
Trube & Kings, Metallbau mbH

Model Maker
Atelier 36 GbR,
Foster and Partners model shop

PA Systems, Telephones
Siemens AG-ANL GT BG

Painting and Coating
Eisenschutz Otto Buchloh,
Brandenburg GmbH

PV Cells
Engotec GmbH

Raised Floors and Screed
Fa. Burkhardt GmbH & Co., Rienth,
Burkhardt, Neunaber

**Restoration—Internal Stone
Façades**
Ellwart Steinrestaurierung

Roof Cladding
Dachdecker GmbH, Schulze & Sohn

Room Control Panels
Weidmüller GmbH + Co

Stone Cladding—Walls and Floors
Kiefer-Reul-Teich Naturstein

Store Reconstruction
FX Rauch KG, Naturstein am Bau

Tiling
Rabe Fliesen-und Marmor-Centrum

**Ventilation, Air Conditioning,
Sprinkler Systems, Plumbing,
Heating**
ARGE Reichstagsgebäudetechnik,
Nickel/WLG/K-U-Z,
Heinrich Nickel GmH

Xenon Lights—Dome
MP Pesch